ANNUAL UPD/  

# DEMOCRACY IN SCOTLAND AND THE UK

for National 5/Higher Modern Studies and Politics

Paul Fairclough
Euan M. Duncan

## Acknowledgements

Every effort has been made to trace all copyright holders, but if any have been inadvertently overlooked, the Publishers will be pleased to make the necessary arrangements at the first opportunity.

Although every effort has been made to ensure that website addresses are correct at time of going to press, Hodder Gibson cannot be held responsible for the content of any website mentioned in this book. It is sometimes possible to find a relocated web page by typing in the address of the home page for a website in the URL window of your browser.

Hachette UK's policy is to use papers that are natural, renewable and recyclable products and made from wood grown in well-managed forests and other controlled sources. The logging and manufacturing processes are expected to conform to the environmental regulations of the country of origin.

Orders: please contact Bookpoint Ltd, 130 Park Drive, Milton Park, Abingdon, Oxon OX14 4SE. Telephone: (44) 01235 827827. Fax: (44) 01235 400401. Email education@bookpoint.co.uk. Lines are open from 9 a.m. to 5 p.m., Monday to Friday, with a 24-hour message answering service. Visit our website at www.hoddereducation.co.uk. If you have queries or questions that aren't about an order, you can contact us at hoddergibson@hodder.co.uk



First published in 2020 by

Hodder Gibson, an imprint of Hodder Education

An Hachette UK Company

211 St Vincent Street

Glasgow, G2 5QY

Impression number 5 4 3 2 1

Year 2024 2023 2022 2021 2020



Typeset in Concorde BQ 9/13 by Integra Software Services Pvt. Ltd., Pondicherry, India

Printed by CPI Group (UK) Ltd, Croydon, CR0 4YY

A catalogue record for this title is available from the British Library.

ISBN: 978 1 5104 6874 0

# Contents

# Contents

# Chapter 1

# Citizens' assemblies: are they a good way to clear political logjams?

## Exam success

The up-to-date facts, examples and arguments in this chapter will help you to produce good-quality answers in the following specification areas:

| NAT5 Modern Studies | Higher Modern Studies | Higher Politics |
| --- | --- | --- |
| • Participation — rights, responsibilities and opportunities for individuals (Scotland)<br>• Power and decision making (Scotland) + (UK)<br>• Representation (Scotland) | • Possible alternatives to the governance of Scotland<br>• Implications of the UK's decision to leave the EU<br>• Ways in which citizens can influence government decision making | • Political systems — constitutional arrangements |

## Context

Whereas most chief executives in other democracies around the world are directly elected, or at least elected in a contest in which all citizens have some kind of input, UK prime ministers hold their position by virtue of the fact that they can command the confidence of the House of Commons. Therefore, with the Conservative Party in government already, Boris Johnson only needed to convince a majority of party members in order to succeed Theresa May as both party leader and prime minister in July 2019. While it is true that a change of prime minister occurring in such circumstances is always contentious, not least because the absence of a general election raises questions about the nature of the new administration's mandate, Johnson also took office at a time of considerable uncertainty regarding both Brexit and the very future of the union of Scotland and England.

In the face of such constitutional flux, many have suggested that citizens' assemblies might be an effective means of affording the government a clearer mandate for action, while at the same time widening political participation. This chapter examines the extent to which citizens' assemblies of the type widely advocated at home and used extensively elsewhere could indeed be useful in clearing political logjams.

In doing so, it will consider the following issues:

- What are citizens' assemblies?
- Where have citizens' assemblies been used previously and to what effect?
- How might citizens' assemblies help to clear political logjams?
- How do citizens' assemblies sit alongside UK democracy?

## What are citizens' assemblies?

Although citizens' assemblies were very much 'in vogue' in 2019, they are hardly novel. Alongside citizens' juries (see Box 1.1) such groupings were mooted in Gordon Brown's Constitutional Renewal Bill 2008–09, and have been used widely since – in one form or another – both in the UK and beyond.

### Box 1.1 Citizens' juries

- a panel of citizens brought together to hear evidence and deliver their verdict on a specific government proposal or area of policy
- used widely outside the UK, most notably in the US and Germany
- a panel of specialists considers the jury's feedback, but politicians have the final say

Citizens' juries and citizens' assemblies are similar in the sense that they look to engage a representative cross section of the population in the policy-making process, in a way that is more meaningful than the kind of consultation that is often undertaken at the Green Paper stage of the legislative process.

However, citizens' assemblies differ from juries in the following ways:

1 They actively involve a lot more people (perhaps hundreds or thousands, as opposed to tens).

2 They generally have the power to decide upon a particular course of action, which can then be formally confirmed by referendum.

Put simply, while elected politicians retain the final say in respect of any proposals arising from a citizens' jury, establishing a citizens' assembly has the potential to entirely remove politicians from the decision-making process (see Box 1.2).

### Box 1.2 The four phases in the lifecycle of a citizens' assembly

1. **1** Selection: members are chosen.
2. **2** Hearings: specialists present evidence.
3. **3** Deliberation: the assembly considers the evidence and their responses to it.
4. **4** Recommendations: the formal proposals are codified and taken forward for approval.

## Where have citizens' assemblies been used previously and to what effect?

The House of Lords' introduction to citizens' assemblies, published in February 2019, provides a clear overview of some of the ways in which such devices have been used in the UK in recent years (see Box 1.3).

### Box 1.3 Recent usages of citizens' assemblies

Assemblies have been set up to consider subjects such as English devolution, adult social care and a range of different matters in Ireland (including abortion laws and climate change). These have been organised by a range of bodies, including think-tanks, academic institutions, parliamentary committees and, in the case of Ireland, the Parliament itself.

**Source:** Taylor, R. (2019) *Citizens' Assemblies: An Introductory Guide*, House of Lords Library Briefing.

**Weblink:** House of Lords Briefing Paper (LLN-2019-0017):
**https://researchbriefings.parliament.uk**

Although most of those assemblies held in the UK have been established by specific institutions, as opposed to by government itself, government-sanctioned assemblies have been used widely elsewhere — for example in Ireland (see Box 1.4).

### Box 1.4 The Irish experience

- The Irish Parliament passed a resolution backing the creation of a citizens' assembly.
- The assembly recommended changes to Ireland's abortion laws.
- The government legislated to approve these changes.
- The changes were confirmed in a referendum held on 25 May 2018.

**Weblink:** The Irish Citizens' Assembly:
**www.citizensassembly.ie/en/**

## How might citizens' assemblies help to clear political logjams?

As we have seen, citizens' assemblies have already been used to address a range of complex and/or intractable problems, both within the UK and further afield. However, the widespread interest in such devices in 2019, as reported in the press, was prompted by the apparent impasse over Brexit in the wake of the Commons' repeated rejection of Theresa May's EU withdrawal agreement, and the possible knock-on effects that this might have in the face of growing support for 'IndyRef2' (a second Scottish independence referendum) in Scotland.

While the experience of the Citizens' Assembly on Brexit, organised by University College London (UCL) in 2017, would suggest there is some mileage in employing assemblies in such circumstances, it is clear that the nature and quality of the process put in place determines just how useful such assemblies might be in clearing the kinds of logjams identified above.

**Weblink:** Citizens' Assembly on Brexit: **www.ucl.ac.uk/constitution-unit**

Discussion for discussion's sake, without any sense of how it might feed into the decision-making process, always runs the risk of feeding political alienation and disaffection, as opposed to combatting it. As Runswick noted in 2007, the best way to ensure that a citizens' assembly is meaningful and effective is firstly to give it real power and secondly to make the process transparent from the outset (see Box 1.5). A failure to deliver on either front is likely to result in the assembly being seen as yet another expensive and fruitless exercise in pseudo-consultation or window dressing.

### Box 1.5 What makes a good citizens' assembly?

- The assembly has to be seen to be independent and have the power to propose change.
- Citizens' assemblies have been successful where it has been established from the outset that their findings will be put straight to a referendum, without government amendment or modification.
- In these cases the assembly was seen to be independent and consequently the public and media bought into the process.
- Where it is not clear what the outcome will be, or the assembly merely reports to Parliament, as in the Netherlands, the assembly is dismissed as 'yet another consultation exercise' that is 'unlikely to lead to change'.

**Source:** Runswick, A. (2007) *A Guide to Involving Citizens in Constitutional Reform*, Unlock Democracy.

## How do citizens' assemblies sit alongside UK democracy?

In common with most Western democracies, the UK has traditionally been characterised as an indirect or 'representative democracy'. The term 'representative democracy' describes a system of government under which citizens elect representatives to enact legislation and take decisions on their behalf (see Box 1.6).

### Box 1.6 The Burkean model of representative democracy

Edmund Burke (1774) summed up the essence of representative democracy when he stated that, 'your representative owes you not his industry only but his judgement, and he betrays you if he sacrifices it to your opinion'.

What this means in practice is that:

- citizens elect individuals to represent their interests in the legislature until the next election
- these elected representatives are not simply delegates and are therefore free to make decisions that are contrary to their constituents' wishes

Employing devices such as citizens' assemblies more widely would effectively be moving the UK towards a more 'consultative' or 'participatory' style of democracy, where a more conventional representative democracy incorporates elements of direct democracy – such as public inquiries, referendums, citizens assemblies or elements of e-democracy – with a view to engaging the broader citizenry in the policy-making process.

While the rise of groups such as Avaaz and 38 Degrees, and the growing popularity of e-petitions, would suggest that there is a public appetite for more direct participation in the decision-making process, going down this road in the absence of a clearly codified constitution could bring significant pitfalls. For example, what kinds of issues would remain within the government's remit and which would be referred to a citizens' assembly, and who would make a final determination?

- Giving the government the right to decide whether or not to refer a matter to the public might run the risk of politicians abdicating their responsibility to govern when faced with electorally risky decisions – or feeling pressured into offering a citizens' assembly due to a rising tide of public opinion.
- Giving judges the right to decide whether or not to refer a matter to the public might run the risk of politicising the judiciary and undermining parliamentary sovereignty.

**Weblink:** the UK government's e-petitions site: **https://petition.parliament.uk/**

## Conclusion

The failure of politicians on all sides to run the 2016 Brexit campaign in a spirit that ensured the public were educated to a level where they could fully appreciate the consequences of any decision they made, and the subsequent failure of parliament to deliver 'the will of the 17 million', naturally prompted a good deal of soul-searching in the years that followed. While politicians have naturally been keen to re-engage with the public at the end of a quarter-century in which participation in formal politics has fallen to historically low levels, the wider use of referendums has done little to satisfy that desire. Indeed, the 2014 and 2016 referendums, on Scottish independence and Brexit respectively, served only to muddy the waters on both questions, fuel resentment on all sides and further undermine public confidence in established democratic institutions.

Where citizens' assemblies offer a way forward, therefore, is because they are a means of having an informed, measured and wide-ranging public discussion in advance of any referendum. They provide the kind of process that might take the heat out of any issue under discussion, challenge myths and misinformation, and pave the way for a public vote in which all parties, however reluctantly, might accept the outcome. The reality, however, is that the wider use of such devices should probably come at the end of a more general debate about the nature of democracy in the UK, of the kind envisaged in the 2020 Citizens' Convention (see weblink below), rather than as a short-term quick-fix when, as in the case of Brexit, Westminster faces political stalemate.

**Weblink:** 'Could you help shape the future of UK democracy?, 30 July 2019: **www.bbc.co.uk**

### Summary

- Declining participation in formal politics and a desire to involve the wider public more directly in decision making has led some to champion the merits of citizens' assemblies.
- Such assemblies, which may involve a representative cross section of hundreds or thousands of citizens, have been used successfully to resolve intractable problems elsewhere.
- Where instituted by a government, such assemblies may be able to make proposals that could be put to a referendum without approval by the government or the legislature.
- Some feel that establishing a citizens' assembly could have provided a way past the stalemate over Brexit.
- The use of such devices could be seen to undermine the nature of representative democracy in the UK.
- Many leading commentators believe that there should be a root and branch debate about the future of UK democracy of the kind proposed in the 2-year Citizens' Convention, launched in January 2020.

### How can I use this information in my exam?

Citizens' assemblies provide an up-to-date example of how citizens can participate in the UK and Scottish governments, as well as in a representative democracy more broadly. This makes them an ideal example to support your answers in SQA examinations. They are relevant to questions that ask you about how citizens participate in UK and Scottish democracy, as well as the ways in which citizens can influence government decision making. Moreover, they can be mentioned in relation to the search for alternatives to the governance of Scotland and managing the implication of the UK's decision to leave the EU.

Successful answers, be it for Modern Studies or Politics, will use detailed evidence from this chapter linked to the exam question with evaluative or analytical language. Strong answers will not simply mention citizens' assemblies but will add rich descriptive language. Using specific and detailed examples of citizens' assemblies, such as when they were formed and where they have operated, will show a greater depth of knowledge, which can then be linked back to the question being asked. You can also comment on the strengths or weaknesses of citizens' assemblies, or give specific examples of successes or limitations – whether in relation to enhancing citizen participation or clearing political logjams.

## Consolidation activities

1. Describe, in detail, what a citizens' assembly is.
2. Give a range of examples of where and when citizens' assemblies have been used.
3. Focus on one specific example of where a citizens' assembly has been used.
   - Describe its aims.
   - Make an assessment on whether or not it was effective in achieving its aims.
   - Use evidence to support your answer.
4. Make a table that lists the strengths and weaknesses of citizens' assemblies.
5. Outline the ways in which the use of citizens' assemblies could be used to enhance democracy in Scotland or the UK as a whole.
6. What implications could a shift towards citizens' assemblies have for the UK's traditional model of representative democracy?

# Chapter 2

# The Scottish Parliament: is it a failing institution?

## Exam success

The up-to-date facts, examples and arguments in this chapter will help you to produce good-quality answers in the following specific areas:

| NAT5 Modern Studies | Higher Modern Studies | Higher Politics |
| --- | --- | --- |
| • Power and decision making (Scotland)<br>• Participation (Scotland)<br>• Representation (Scotland) | • Possible alternatives for the governance of Scotland<br>• Implications of the UK's decision to leave the EU<br>• Effectiveness of parliamentary representatives in holding the government to account<br>• Strengths and weaknesses of different electoral systems in the UK | • Political theory — power, authority and legitimacy<br>• Political theory — democracy<br>• Political systems — the legislative branch and the executive branch |

## Context

2019 marked two decades of governance by the Scottish Parliament in Holyrood, and was therefore an apt time to reflect on the relative success of the parliament in the period since its grand opening in 1999. The public debate that followed included comments by former secretary of state for Scotland David Mundell who, in an interview with the independent think-tank 'Reform Scotland', argued that the Scottish Parliament had neither fulfilled its potential, nor lived up to the founding idea of the parliament. Much of this criticism centred around the argued limitations of the Scottish committee system, the failure to improve in key policy areas such as education (see Chapter 6), the inability to break away from 'Westminster style' party politics, and what some would view as a tendency to focus on an excessively narrow constitutional agenda. However, Mundell's view is not shared by all, with some instead pointing to the argued successes of the parliament, whether it be the introduction of key social democratic policies such as free personal care and bus passes for the elderly, UK-leading rights provision on several LGBT+ issues, or health policies such as the smoking ban, the introduction of minimum unit pricing for alcohol, and the willingness to continue funding free eye and dental checks north of the border.

This chapter will look at the supposed successes and failures of the parliament, with a view to allowing a judgement to be made as to whether or not it is fair to conclude that the Scottish Parliament is indeed a failing institution.

In doing so, it will consider the following issues:

- In what ways could the Scottish Parliament be seen as 'failing'?
- In what ways could the Scottish Parliament be seen as operating 'effectively'?

## In what ways could the Scottish Parliament be seen as 'failing'?

### 1 The committee system

When the Scottish Parliament opened in 1999, the committee system was much vaunted. Indeed, it was supposed to be the institution's 'crowning jewel'. Committees are especially important in the Scottish Parliament: since it is a unicameral legislature without an upper house to check and review its work, committees provide the primary means of scrutinising legislative proposals. Scottish committees are something of a hybrid in that they sit somewhere between the kinds of standing committees and select committees that operate at Westminster (see Box 2.1). Crucially, Scottish committees have no elected convener.

**Box 2.1 What do committees do in the Scottish Parliament?**

- Committees scrutinise the work of the Scottish Parliament, including the scrutiny of budget proposals.
- They hold enquiries into subjects relating to the work of the committee.
- They examine legislation, including bills and subordinate legislation.
- They consider petitions that have been submitted.

**Weblink:** The role of committees in the Scottish Parliament: **www.parliament.scot**

Though such 'hybrid' committees are similar in many ways to those operating in other Western democracies, most notably in the US, some feel that the committee system as a whole has failed to live up to initial expectations. One of the criticisms of the system is that the committees have, as yet, failed to make the most of the powers granted to them. For example, in Scotland, committees have the power to introduce legislation, yet this has been used rarely. Moreover, conveners (i.e. the committee 'chairs') are not elected as in Westminster, but selected by political parties. This can be seen as a limitation, as it allows political parties to influence committees more, rather than encouraging independent work and cross-party collaboration.

Another limitation cited is the small number of Members of the Scottish Parliament (MSPs) who are available to serve on these all important Committees. With no upper chamber, committees are vital in scrutinising all legislation, yet there are only 129 MSPs. This difference is particularly stark, as not only does Westminster have the scrutiny of the House of Lords but also around 650 MPs available to work on committees. Having such a small number of MSPs can lead either to an insurmountable workload or, at the very least, less time to scrutinise individual pieces of legislation fully, potentially reducing the robustness and efficiency of laws passed in the parliament. According to Tricia Marwick, the former presiding officer of the parliament, the jury is still out on the committee system.

### 2 The 'same old politics'

When the Scottish Parliament opened, much was made of the fact that it was to champion a new style of politics. This was to involve a departure from the so-called traditional 'tribal party politics' that were seen as a negative aspect of politics south of the border, and instead promote collaboration, coalitions and consensus. This was the principle behind the design of the chamber itself, which uses a horseshoe shape meant to contrast starkly with the opposition benches two sword-lengths apart in Westminster. There has been criticism that the Scottish Parliament has not achieved a new style of politics, and in fact party discipline is as tight and rigid in Scotland as it is in Westminster. Indeed, David Mundell also mentioned in his comment for Reform Scotland that it was this that was holding back the work of the Scottish Parliament, as MSPs were failing to distinguish between their roles as politicians and parliamentarians.

**Weblink:** 'Devolution at 20: why Holyrood has still to forge its own identity' by David Mundell, 3 June 2019: **https://reformscotland.com**

The *Observer* journalist Neal Ascherson supports this, arguing that the true failure of the Scottish Parliament was its inability to break away from tribal Westminster-style politics. According to the former first minister Henry McLeish, this has the effect that even though MSPs across party lines agree most of the time, it is often the few differences that are emphasised, for party political gain. Therefore the Scottish Parliament has, in effect, failed to break away from traditional politics, and perhaps failed to live up to the expectations many held for it in this regard.

## In what ways could the Scottish Parliament be seen as operating 'effectively'?

### 1 Social legislation

The Scottish Parliament has acted boldly on key social policies, often in the face of significant opposition, and been willing to lead the way in several significant policy areas. One such area is healthcare. Key policies include the ban on smoking in public places in 2006, the provision of free personal care to all under the Community Care Act 2019 and free bus travel for the over 60s. This has accompanied a broader social agenda, headlined with Scotland becoming the first country in the UK to ban the smacking of children. This has all occurred alongside the introduction of minimum unit pricing for alcohol and the relatively quick introduction of laws designed to promote greater equality on LGBT+ issues, such as the repeal of Section 28, which banned the discussion of homosexuality in schools. Nicola Sturgeon mentioned many of these initiatives in a speech on 7 July

2019 in which she reflected on 20 years of the Scottish Parliament. 'From land reform in the first parliament, to equal marriage in the last, to the Social Security Act [2018] in this', she noted, 'they have all made Scotland a better place'. Many have heralded the fact that the Scottish Parliament has been able to promote a more equal, fair and tolerant society as a success. This achievement was perhaps especially impressive in that the government often clashed with powerful interests in the pursuit of this type of society, such as powerful investors like Sir Brian Souter and his high-profile 'Keep the Clause' campaign.

Additionally, this touches on another argued strength of the parliament. According to the former first minister Henry McLeish, who was speaking at a politics festival event in June 2019, one of the main successes of the parliament has been its ability to legislate on Scottish issues with MSPs drawing up and scrutinising legislation. His point revolves around what he called the 'tremendous backlog' of required legislation needed to improve things in Scotland, given that little time had been set aside on the Westminster legislative agenda prior to the opening of parliament. In fact, over 200 pieces of legislation have been passed, pointing to the ability of the parliament to legislate effectively on Scottish issues.

### 2 Successful integration into Scottish society

Another arguable success of the parliament is that it has quickly and successfully established itself as Scotland's parliament. This should not necessarily be taken for granted, as other political decisions that involve constitutional change have generated huge controversy and division. Polling suggests that Scots accept that the Scottish Parliament is the main legislature for Scotland, and that they trust it to do that job. This was made clear in a survey for 'What Scotland Thinks', where 60% of respondents said that they trusted the Scottish Parliament, whereas only 20% of respondents said that they trusted Westminster. This was reinforced with results from the Scottish Social Attitudes (SSA) survey of 2018 (see Box 2.2).

#### Box 2.2 Findings of the 2018 Scottish Social Attitudes (SSA) survey

- 61% trusted the Scottish government to work in Scotland's best interests compared with 20% for the UK government.
- Nearly three-quarters believed the Scottish government ought to have most influence over the way Scotland is run compared with 15% who said the UK government should.
- Of those who said the standard of living had worsened over the past 12 months, 50% attributed this to UK government policy, whereas 16% attributed this to Scottish government policy.
- Of those who said the standard of living had improved over the past 12 months, 43% attributed this to Scottish government policy, whereas 28% attributed this to UK government policy.

**Weblink:** 'Public trust in the Scottish government', 26 June 2018: **https://news.gov.scot**

The fact that the Scottish Parliament is trusted, respected and credited with improving people's lives in Scotland must surely be viewed as a success for this young and developing institution.

Connected to this has been the argument that the parliament is open, representative and accessible. This has a practical element too, as today over half of the population of Scotland are within one hour's travel of the parliament, and it is therefore physically more accessible. Moreover, the parliament has focused on engaging young people in politics, be it through the Youth Parliament or, since 2015, implementing a voting age of 16 for parliament and local government elections.

Finally, some argue that the Scottish electoral system is evidence that the Scottish Parliament is more representative than Westminster. The additional member system of voting is a hybrid between first past the post and proportional representation, so smaller parties are represented in parliament. This allows for a fairer allocation of MSPs within parliament and gives voters more choice in elections.

**Weblink:** Results of the 2016 Scottish Parliament elections: **www.bbc.co.uk/news/election/2016/scotland/results**

## Conclusion

The late Donald Dewar famously said that, 'Devolution is not an event, it is a process', and agreement seems to exist around the idea that the Scottish Parliament has successfully integrated into Scottish political life. The warnings from Whitehall in the late 1990s, that if Scotland were to gain control of major policy areas such as health or education it would invariably lead to disaster, have not been borne out.

We should remember that the creation of the Scottish Parliament in 1999 was the biggest constitutional change in the UK since the division of Ireland in 1922. Yet, unlike other constitutional challenges such as Brexit (see Chapter 5), it occurred with a minimum of fuss or controversy.

As the journalist Paul Hutcheon noted, the Scottish Parliament is still young, and it would therefore take something of a cynic to classify it as a failing institution just two decades in. It may simply be that the parliament has not, as yet, lived up to the lofty hopes and expectations that many onlookers had for the legislature at the time of its creation.

## Summary

- A criticism of the parliament has been that the committee system is not strong enough to effectively scrutinise legislation.
- Committees are especially important in Scotland since there is no upper house, yet they have not effectively used their powers.
- The parliament can almost be seen as being 'under-staffed', with only 129 MSPs and a significant quantity of legislation to process.
- Generally speaking, Scotland has been unable to break away from traditional party politics.
- The Scottish Parliament has produced large quantities of legislation that some argue has made Scotland a better place to live.
- The Scottish Parliament has become an integrated part of Scottish life and there are no serious calls to return to direct rule.

## How can I use this information in my exam?

This information can be used directly when talking about the governance of Scotland and to weigh up the successes and failures of parliament. When you are giving answers, ensure that you use specific examples and facts to support your points, as this will help you to gain all available marks. Focus on specific areas such as the committee system, and consider researching this further. For the study of politics, this section provides clear evidence of a legislature at work, and can be used as an example of a democratic system.

## Consolidation activities

1. Draw up a table listing all of the ways in which the Scottish Parliament could be seen as 'effective' and 'ineffective'.
   Study your completed table carefully and answer the following questions:
   a. Select one argument on the 'effective' side of the debate and use your own research to produce a mini case study that illustrates the point in question.
   b. Select one argument on the 'ineffective' side of the debate and use your own research to produce a mini case study that illustrates the point in question.
2. Describe, in detail, the committee system that operates within the Scottish Parliament.
3. Conduct research on one mandatory committee and do the following:
   a. Give a brief overview of its composition and areas of responsibility.
   b. Give a recent example of its work.
4. Conduct research on one subject committee and do the following:
   a. Give a brief overview of its composition and areas of responsibility.
   b. Give a recent example of its work.

# Chapter 3

# Extinction Rebellion: do single-issue pressure groups undermine democracy?

## Exam success

The up-to-date facts, examples and arguments in this chapter will help you to produce good-quality answers in the following specification areas:

| NAT5 Modern Studies | Higher Modern Studies | Higher Politics |
|---|---|---|
| • Influence — pressure groups (Scotland) + (UK)<br>• Participation (Scotland) + (UK)<br>• Power and decision making (UK) | • Ways in which citizens can influence government decision making, including pressure groups | • Political systems |

## Context

In April 2019, Extinction Rebellion, a group formed a year earlier, staged a series of public demonstrations in London and in major cities across the UK — something it repeated in August 2019, and again in October, in the form of the group's 2-week 'uprising'. For some, this was a watershed moment in the environmental movement, with student-led strikes in many parts of the country resulting in widespread school closures, non-violent direct action causing significant disruption in many cities, and leading politicians across party lines rushing to declare a 'climate emergency'.

However, while some saw this as largely a positive development in terms of political participation, not least because so many young people were involved in the protests, others questioned whether the rise of such media-savvy populist movements, far from reinvigorating representative democracy, might in fact serve only to undermine it further.

This chapter offers a brief overview of the Extinction Rebellion phenomenon before moving on to question how comfortably such single-issue pressure group campaigns sit alongside traditional representative institutions and associated processes.

In doing so, it will consider the following issues:

- What factors have led to the emergence of groups such as Extinction Rebellion?
- In what ways can the activities of groups like Extinction Rebellion be seen as a 'good thing'?
- In what ways can the activities of groups like Extinction Rebellion be seen as a 'bad thing'?
- What does the rise of Extinction Rebellion tell us about the state of UK politics?

## What factors have led to the emergence of groups such as Extinction Rebellion?

Recent years have witnessed the rise of a 'new pressure group politics' far removed from the traditional mass-membership groups that once provided the main focus of study for students of UK politics.

In the latter half of the twentieth century, successful pressure groups were often characterised by the existence of formal organisation and membership structures. This was because such features were necessary, both for the group to operate and to survive for any length of time, and for the government to view the group as being legitimate. Crucially, groups needed money to finance their campaigns and, for most groups, this necessitated the stable income stream provided by annual membership fees. New entrants to the game of pressure group politics were disadvantaged both by the absence of some or all of these positive features and by their inability to access the information they needed in order to mount credible and authoritative campaigns. This, after all, was an age in which access to and control of knowledge was a key feature of power.

In recent years, however, a number of fundamental changes in politics and society have served to change the landscape of UK pressure group politics, thereby bringing into question many long-held assumptions (see Box 3.1).

### Box 3.1 A changing society

- The emergence of a 24-hour mass media created an ongoing demand for news stories and 'good visuals' that opened the door to high-profile stunts and other forms of low-cost yet impactful direct action.
- The growth of more affordable and more immediate methods of communication reduced the 'cost of entry' for new groups, thereby removing the need for traditional membership structures and fees.
- The advent of the 'information age' provided for a democratisation of knowledge, accompanied by a greater commitment to freedom of information, allowing groups to get the information they needed in order to operate more effectively and to therefore speak with greater authority.

### Key concepts

Direct action:

- highly visible forms of protest, often involving physical non-violent action or civil disobedience
- often seeking to attract local or national media coverage as a means of raising awareness and furthering the cause in question

Civil disobedience:

- the act of refusing certain orders given by the state, without resorting to physical violence
- closely associated with the 'non-violence' of political leaders such as Mahatma Gandhi in India, and Martin Luther King, Jr. in the USA

The cumulative effect of these changes has been to make it far easier for people to campaign without the kind of formal pressure group organisation and structure once considered essential to success. Such developments have, at the same time, greatly reduced the relative advantage of those groups that once relied heavily on their financial resources as a means of exerting their political influence.

Moreover, whereas embryonic groups might once have had to campaign for some considerable time before the media picked up on them or the government of the day acknowledged and granted them 'access', loosely organised groups, or networks of related groups, are now able to emerge and mount credible campaigns with great speed. Such groups have the added advantage that their mode of operation makes it far harder for their opponents (or the authorities) to target them or disrupt their activities. Extinction Rebellion (see Box 3.2) is just such a group.

### Box 3.2 Extinction Rebellion

**Founded:** May 2018

**Description:**

- Extinction Rebellion (XR) is a decentralised and loosely organised grassroots network.
- Anyone who takes non-violent action in support of its stated goals, and in line with its ten principles, can claim to do it in the name of XR.

**Stated principles and values:**

- We have a shared vision of change, creating a world that is fit for generations to come.
- We set our mission on what is necessary.
- We need a regenerative culture.
- We openly challenge ourselves and our toxic system.
- We value reflecting and learning.
- We welcome everyone and every part of everyone.
- We actively mitigate for power, breaking down hierarchies of power for more equitable participation.
- We avoid blaming and shaming.
- We are a non-violent network.
- We are based on autonomy and decentralisation.

**Methods:**

- In its own words, 'Extinction Rebellion is an international movement that uses non-violent civil disobedience in an attempt to halt mass extinction and minimise the risk of social collapse.'

**Weblink:** **https://rebellion.earth**

**Weblink:** 'Who are Extinction Rebellion and what do they want? BBC Newsround, 15 October 2019: **www.bbc.co.uk**

## In what ways can the activities of groups like Extinction Rebellion be seen as a 'good thing'?

While many would naturally see the activities of Extinction Rebellion as a 'good thing', because of the serious and immediate threat facing the environment, we are choosing to focus more on the extent to which the group's aims, approaches and methods sit comfortably alongside the processes and principles that have traditionally underpinned the UK system of government.

The UK is traditionally seen as a representative democracy (see Box 3.3). While its systems have always allowed a degree of pressure group access, therefore, there has been a tendency in government to favour engagement with more established insider groups, as opposed to being 'bounced' into decisions by the kinds of mass public protests that outsider groups commonly organise.

### Box 3.3 Representative democracy

- In a representative democracy the people elect someone to represent them in a legislative body.
- The nature of the representation can take many forms but essentially the elected representatives debate and discuss laws on behalf of the people who have elected them.
- The elected representative/s may act on what their constituents want or on what they think would be best for their constituents, or they may represent wider groups when debating and creating laws.

**Source:** Lynch, P., Fairclough, P., Cooper, T. (2017) *UK Government and Politics for AS/A-Level*, Philip Allan.

That said, in the face of historically low levels of participation in formal politics in the early part of the twenty-first century, many have come to see movements such as Extinction Rebellion as a positive development, given that they do, at least, serve to draw people into politics and encourage them to engage with the 'big issues' – as can be seen in the reported 28% surge in the numbers of pupils applying to study politics at undergraduate level.

If nothing else, the strength of public feeling demonstrated by mass protests of the kinds organised by groups such as the Stop the War Coalition, in 2003, and

The People's Vote and Extinction Rebellion, in 2019, give the government a clear steer on the kinds of issues that people care about.

**Weblink:** **https://peoples-vote.uk**

## In what ways can the activities of groups like Extinction Rebellion be seen as 'a bad thing'?

It was the former foreign secretary Douglas Hurd who once described pressure groups as 'serpents that strangle efficient government', and one can see how the activities of groups such as Extinction Rebellion might receive such criticism. For instance:

- Mass demonstrations and civil disobedience may cause a level of disruption and expense that is out of all proportion to the merit of a given cause or the level of support it receives.
- Vocal single-issue campaigns sometimes make it harder for the government of the day to focus on meeting the needs of all citizens and establishing appropriate priorities.

It is clear that the climate change strikes organised in Extinction Rebellion's name gained significant traction, both with those school-age children who joined them and the wider public. However, the disruption some of the group's activities caused divided opinion. In the wake of the April protests, the Commissioner of the Metropolitan Police Cressida Dick claimed that there had been an additional £7.5 million in related costs to the force – and, by implication, to the taxpayer (see Box 3.4). The protests in October, which included disruption of the London Underground (see Box 3.5), also raised questions about the legitimacy of such forms of protest.

### Box 3.4 Police sought tougher powers against Extinction Rebellion

- Government and police discussed strengthening public order laws to allow a tougher crackdown on future Extinction Rebellion demonstrations.
- Changes to specific sections of the Public Order Act 1986 were discussed.
- The move came as XR's 2-week 'uprising' drew to a close on Friday 18 October.
- The Metropolitan Police had earlier faced criticism after officers implemented a city-wide ban on the protests.
- The Met said more than 1,700 people had been arrested for taking part in the XR protests.
- Thousands of people blocked roads, glued themselves to government buildings and blockaded big financial institutions to raise the alarm about the escalating climate emergency.
- One group targeted the London Underground network.

**Source:** *Guardian*, 19 October 2019

## Box 3.5 The Extinction Rebellion tube protest

Senior figures in Extinction Rebellion (XR) admit it was a mistake to target London's public transport network at rush hour, a move that has split opinion within the movement. Future strategy is now being reassessed, they say.

At the end of the 2-week global 'uprising', members of the movement's political circle announced that it needed to learn from the angry scenes at Canning Town tube station last Thursday when commuters dragged protesters from the roof of an underground train and set upon them. Eight XR activists were arrested during the disruption, joining a total of 1,768 held during the fortnight of demonstrations.

British Transport Police confirmed it was also investigating and looking to acquire evidence against a number of commuters who appeared to embark on a vigilante-style attack on one of the Canning Town protesters.

**Source:** *Guardian*, Sunday 20 October 2019

## What does the rise of Extinction Rebellion tell us about the state of UK politics?

### The end of ideology

Although we have already identified some of the reasons why less formal pressure group movements such as Extinction Rebellion have flourished in recent years, it is clear that they have also benefited from a breakdown in the traditional 'left' versus 'right' ideological divide that characterised British party politics for much of the twentieth century. In a political landscape increasingly driven by questions of 'identity' and how people 'feel', as opposed to long-term adherence to an ideological creed, issues such as the environment and Brexit have emerged as populist causes that cut across traditional party lines. Involvement in such informal and disparate movements may also seem more immediate and more engaging to those disillusioned by more traditional forms of participation.

### Political culture

In the same way that historic ideological divisions have declined as a factor shaping pressure group activity, so the recalibration of the UK's political culture has made it easier for populists and those at the margins to gain leverage. Where UK political culture was traditionally framed by the existence of consensus, homogeneity and deference, all of these defining characteristics have lost currency since the 1980s – even at the heart of government. For example, while an acceptance of the notion of parliamentary government and the rule of law would have once made it inconceivable that a UK prime minister could even consider breaking the law, Boris Johnson was able to remain in office despite having been found to have acted unlawfully in respect of his prorogation advice to the queen, and continue to govern even when he was accused of deliberately setting out to undermine the purpose of the European Union (Withdrawal) (No. 2) Act 2019, the so-called 'Benn Act'.

## Key concepts

Political culture:

- the opinions, attitudes and values that shape political behaviour
- a nation's political culture consists of the citizens' collectively held attitudes towards the political system and their place in it

### Summary

- Recent years have seen the rise of a number of less formal and more disparate political movements, such as Extinction Rebellion.
- Traditional pressure groups were generally hierarchical in structure, with permanent organisation and paid-up members.
- These new groups are often little more than networks of independent activists who agree to follow a simple set of guiding principles or aims in order to operate under the movement's 'umbrella'.
- Although many feel that the rise of such groups has been a positive development in an age in which participation in formal politics has been in decline, others argue that their activities undermine representative democracy.
- The rise of such informal movements reflects significant changes in UK society and political culture.

### How can I use this information in my exam?

An understanding of the changing nature of pressure group activity as it relates to decision-making and the political system as a whole is obviously a topic that cuts across NAT5 Modern Studies and Higher Modern Studies and Politics. The references to the changing nature of UK society and political culture contained in this chapter are also worthy of note, because they will have a bearing on many other aspects of your studies.

Although we have seen that Extinction Rebellion is not the first of these new pressure group movements to emerge, it is an excellent and current example of how such groups operate as an 'umbrella' for those who subscribe to their cause. Use the group as a case study and undertake your own research to identify specific examples of the kinds of things the group is doing between now and your final examination.

### Consolidation activities

1. Produce a spider diagram which shows the factors that have led to the rise of groups such as Extinction Rebellion.
2. Argue the case in favour of groups such as Extinction Rebellion being allowed to protest in the way that they have been doing in recent years.
3. Argue the case against groups such as Extinction Rebellion being allowed to protest in the way that they have been doing in recent years.
4. Study the excerpt from the *Guardian* article in Box 3.5 (see page 23). What does this tell us about the way in which Extinction Rebellion operates?
5. In your opinion, should there be any limits on the right of groups like Extinction Rebellion to engage in non-violent civil disobedience?

# Chapter 4

# Scottish electoral systems: are they fit for purpose?

**Exam success**

The up-to-date facts, examples and arguments in this chapter will help you to produce good-quality answers in the following specification areas:

| NAT5 Modern Studies | Higher Modern Studies | Higher Politics |
|---|---|---|
| • Representation (Scotland)<br>• Participation (Scotland)<br>• Voting systems — key features and outcomes | • Strengths and weaknesses of different electoral systems used within the UK<br>• Ways in which citizens can influence government decision making | • Political theory — democracy; power, authority and legitimacy<br>• Political parties and elections — theories of voting behaviour |

**Context**

In November 2019, Scottish voters were readying themselves for a third UK-wide general election in just 5 years. This was a contest that would inevitably be shaped both by the vagaries of the first-past-the-post (FPTP) system, and an appetite for tactical voting that had grown significantly in the face of the increasing polarisation characterising 'Brexit Britain'. Important as that election was, however, it is worth noting that most other elections north of the border no longer operate under FPTP. Moreover, most contests in Scotland now take place under a far wider franchise than that which applies in elections to the Westminster Parliament.

This chapter offers a brief overview of the electoral systems currently used in elections in Scotland, before moving on to question of whether or not such systems can be seen as 'fit for purpose' within their given contexts.

In doing so, it will consider the following issues:

- What electoral systems are used in Scotland?
- How does an electoral system impact an election?
- Government reviews of voting systems
- Calls to change electoral systems

## What electoral systems are used in Scotland?

Although voters in Scotland are still asked to cast their ballots under FPTP when voting in elections to the Westminster Parliament, other systems are in use in other contests north of the border. Local elections operate under a proportional representation (PR) system known as single transferrable vote (STV). Members of the Scottish Parliament (MSPs) are elected to the Scottish Parliament at

Holyrood using a hybrid additional member system (AMS), under which some representatives are chosen under FPTP and others are chosen as a 'top-up', using a PR party list system (see Box 4.1).

**Box 4.1 Scottish electoral systems**

- UK Parliament elections: first past the post (FPTP)
- Scottish Parliament elections: additional member system (AMS)
- Scottish local councils: single transferrable vote (STV)

This seemingly complex mix of voting methods (see Box 4.2) provides interesting areas of comparison, in terms of fairness for example, while also allowing us to consider the extent to which electoral outcomes are shaped by the very systems under which different contests operate.

**Box 4.2 Who can vote in Scottish elections in 2019?**

- Scottish Parliament: 16+ British, Irish, EU or qualifying Commonwealth citizens
- Scottish local elections: 16+ British, Irish, EU or qualifying Commonwealth citizens
- UK general election: 18+ British, Irish or qualifying Commonwealth citizens

### 1 Elections to the Westminster Parliament

In common with electorates across the UK, Scottish voters use FPTP when selecting the individual who will represent them as a Member of Parliament (MP) at Westminster. Each of the 59 parliamentary constituencies in Scotland returns a single MP to Westminster, and the SNP dominated these contests at the 2019 general election, winning 48 of the 59 seats available (see Table 4.1).

***Table 4.1 Results of the 2019 (2017) UK general election, Scottish seats only***

| Party | Vote (%) | Seats won (%) | Seats won (59) |
|---|---|---|---|
| SNP | 45.0 (36.9) | 81.4 (59.3) | 48 (35) |
| Labour | 18.6 (27.1) | 1.7 (11.8) | 1 (7) |
| Conservative | 25.1 (28.6) | 10.2 (22.0) | 6 (13) |
| Liberal Democrats | 9.5 (6.8) | 6.8 (6.8) | 4 (4) |
| Scottish turnout | 68.1 (66.4) | | |

### 2 Scottish Parliament elections

Elections to the Scottish Parliament operate under a 'hybrid' AMS system. What that means in practice is that voters are able to cast two ballots, one to elect the individual who will represent their Holyrood constituency, and a second for a political party. The second vote takes place under a PR party list system using larger, regional constituencies. The results in these regional contests are then used to 'top up' parties with a view to delivering a parliament the composition of which more accurately reflects the proportion of votes achieved by each party. The 2016 Scottish Parliament elections saw the SNP win the most seats, although it fell just short of an overall majority, with the support of 44.1% of the votes. Average turnout across all constituencies increased from 50.4% in 2011 to 55.7% in 2016 (see Table 4.2).

***Table 4.2 Results of the 2016 Scottish Parliament elections (parties winning seats)***

| Party | Constituency | | Regional | | Total | |
|---|---|---|---|---|---|---|
| | Vote (%) | Seats (73) | Vote (%) | Seats (56) | Vote (%) | Seats (129) |
| SNP | 46.5 | 59 | 41.7 | 4 | 44.1 | 63 |
| Conservatives | 22.5 | 7 | 22.9 | 24 | 22.5 | 31 |
| Labour | 20.8 | 3 | 22.6 | 21 | 20.8 | 24 |
| Liberal Democrats | 7.8 | 4 | 5.2 | 1 | 6.5 | 5 |
| Green | 0.6 | 0 | 6.6 | 6 | 3.6 | 6 |

### 3 Scottish local council elections

Scottish local council elections operate under the single transferable vote (STV) system. This PR system requires voters to rank candidates in order of preference, as they see fit, with those achieving a certain number of votes (the 'quota') being elected. In the 2017 Scottish local elections, the SNP won a majority of seats, with the Conservative Party displacing Labour as the second biggest party in local councils (see Box 4.3). Turnout was 46.9% (up 7.3% from 2012).

**Box 4.3 Results of the 2017 Scottish local council elections**

- SNP: 32.3% of first preference votes, 35.1% of seats
- Conservative: 25.3% of first preference votes, 22.5% of seats
- Labour: 20.2% of first preference votes, 21.4% of seats
- Liberal Democrats: 6.9% of first preference votes, 5.5% of seats
- Greens: 4.1% of first preference votes, 1.6% of seats

## How does an electoral system impact an election?

One source of debate among commentators is the extent to which the electoral system in place in a given contest affects the electoral outcome. Based on the results above, certain conclusions may be drawn. For example, at the 2017 general election the Conservatives and the Labour Party won around the same share of the vote in Scotland, yet the Conservatives won nearly twice as many seats as Labour.

Such an outcome would certainly suggest that the way in which FPTP operates has a significant impact on electoral outcomes, by penalising those parties whose support is spread out geographically and awarding a 'winner's bonus' to those who can establish regional strongholds. Put simply, FPTP clearly results in outcomes that are massively disproportionate to the percentage of votes secured by each party in Scotland. Indeed, when one compares such results to the far more proportional outcomes achieved in elections to the Scottish Parliament under AMS just a year earlier (see Table 4.2), the impact of electoral systems becomes even more apparent. The 2017 Scottish local council elections held under STV delivered similarly proportional outcomes (see Box 4.3), with a close correlation between the proportion of first preference votes secured and the number of seats won.

Another area where proponents of PR have argued there will be a significant impact of the system on the election is in terms of voter turnout: the suggestion being that voters are more motivated to turn out to vote knowing that a vote cast under a proportional system will be more likely to 'make a difference'. While this would not appear to be borne out by the examples provided in this chapter, one should remember that turnout always tends to get a boost at national and UK-wide contests, where the stakes are seen as being higher. A more meaningful and favourable comparison, perhaps, could be drawn between the 2017 Scottish local election turnout and turnouts achieved in similar contests under FPTP in English local elections held in 2016–18.

**Weblink:** House of Commons briefing on turnout at local elections, 27 July 2017: **https://researchbriefings.files.parliament.uk**

## Government review of voting systems

As we have seen, calls to replace or modify the FPTP system centre on the potential advantages that another system might bring. Those who oppose the wider use of PR systems, in contrast, often point to the greater likelihood of coalition administrations being required, with 29 of the 32 Scottish councils elected under STV in 2017 ending up with no single party in overall control. Other critics cite potential voter confusion, questioning whether employing new systems really does result in the kind of radical transformation in popular politics that the advocates of PR claim for it.

It is perhaps significant that the latest full review of the different voting systems across the UK took place in 2008, more than a decade ago. Moreover, that Ministry of Justice report hardly provided a compelling case in favour of further reform, concluding that there was no clear causal relationship between PR and those key outcomes desired, such as rising electoral turnout or an increase in the numbers of women candidates being returned to office.

## Calls to change electoral systems

The run-up to the 2019 general election saw renewed calls for electoral reform. On 14 November, a number of leading Labour figures and supporters of the

'Make Votes Matter' campaign called on the party to commit to introducing PR in elections to the Westminster Parliament (see weblink below).

**Weblink:** 'Labour should fight for electoral reform', 14 November 2019: **www.theguardian.com**

Leading figures from the other side of the political divide, most notably former home secretary Amber Rudd, also lent their support to such calls. Addressing the think-tank 'Reform', Rudd questioned whether the current FPTP system was 'fit for purpose', arguing that a more proportional system could result in a situation where individuals and political institutions were more likely to respect the results of elections. It is worth noting that the Liberal Democrats have long argued for the introduction of STV for both local and UK parliamentary elections (see Table 4.3), with the SNP and UKIP also supporting the wider use of more proportional systems.

***Table 4.3 Labour and Liberal Democrat manifesto pledges on elections, 2019***

| Labour Manifesto | Liberal Democrat Manifesto |
|---|---|
| Repeal the Fixed-term Parliaments Act 2011 | Introduce STV for UK general elections and English local council elections |
| Lower voting age to 16 | Lower the voting age to 16 |
| Extend full voting rights to all UK residents and introduce automatic voter registration | Extend full voting rights to all EU citizens who have lived in the UK for at least 5 years |

In spite of such arguments, however, there have been few calls to reform the UK system of FPTP from within government in recent years. This is perhaps unsurprising, given that government ministers can hardly be expected to prioritise the reform of the very system that returned their own party to government. The 67.9% 'no' vote in the 2011 AV Referendum – albeit rejecting a system that is 'majoritarian' as opposed to 'PR' – could also be said to have taken the wind out of the sails of those parliamentarians who had previously pushed for electoral reform.

**Weblink:** House of Commons briefing on electoral systems, 26 October 2017: **https://researchbriefings.parliament.uk**

## Conclusion

The experience of voters using a range of electoral systems in Scotland would appear to suggest that those systems employing a proportional element do indeed deliver 'fairer' outcomes, although without necessarily increasing electoral turnout. However, it is important to remember that an ability to deliver a degree of proportionality is only one of a number of ways of assessing the relative merits of different electoral systems, and perhaps not even the most important.

## Summary

- Voters in Scotland use FPTP to elect MPs in the UK Parliament, a hybrid AMS system to elect MSPs in the Scottish Parliament, and STV to elect local councillors.
- PR electoral systems appear to result in outcomes that more accurately reflect the breakdown of votes cast.
- PR systems more commonly result in minority governments or coalitions.
- Using a PR electoral system does not necessarily guarantee higher turnout.
- There has been little appetite among successive Westminster governments to reform the FPTP electoral system that saw them returned to office.
- Irrespective of the systems used in different contests, the SNP remains the largest party representing Scotland in the UK Parliament, the Scottish Parliament and local government.

## How can I use this information in my exam?

This information will be useful when studying the nature and impact of different electoral systems. Use the data to make developed points about participation, representation and voting behaviour. Reflect on how you can use the data to compare the systems, so drawing out the advantages and disadvantages of each. Remember to make your basic points before selecting and deploying examples and data to show development.

## Consolidation activities

1. Describe, in detail, how the first-past-the-post (FPTP) electoral system operates in relation to UK general elections.
2. Describe, in detail, the additional member system (AMS) used to elect MSPs to the Scottish Parliament.
3. Answer **one** of the following questions:
   a. Make a table listing the 'advantages' and 'disadvantages' of each of the three main electoral systems discussed in this chapter. Remember to use specific examples in support.
   b. Produce a large spider diagram that describes each of the three main electoral systems covered in this chapter, while also covering the impact (or potential impact) that each system may have on electoral outcomes.

   It might help to think about the following 'desirables' when completing this task:
   - voter choice
   - proportionality
   - MP–constituency link
   - stable government
4. Re-read this chapter and any other notes that you have on STV. Using real-world examples to support the points that you make:
   a. Write a letter to a Westminster MP setting out the case in favour of the introduction of STV in elections to the Westminster Parliament.
   b. Write a response from an MP arguing why that would not be desirable.

hapter 5

# Brexit: is it the UK's constitutional time-bomb?

## Exam success

The up-to-date facts, examples and arguments in this chapter will help you to produce good-quality answers in the following specification areas:

| NAT5 Modern Studies | Higher Modern Studies | Higher Politics |
|---|---|---|
| • Participation (UK)<br>• Influence (UK)<br>• Representation — purpose, function and composition of the House of Lords (UK) | • Possible alternatives to the governance of Scotland<br>• Implications of the UK's decision to leave the EU | • Political systems — constitutional arrangements<br>• Political theory — power, authority and legitimacy<br>• Political parties and elections — the dominant ideas within political parties |

## Context

In August 2019 it was widely reported that the UK might well face 'food chaos' in the event of a so-called 'no-deal Brexit', with supermarket shelves left empty and fresh produce in short supply. Just a week earlier, the governor of the Bank of England, Mark Carney, had warned of an 'instant shock' if the UK left the EU with no deal at the end of October, with soaring prices for fuel and food bringing about a 'real-terms' reduction in incomes. 'The economics of no deal are that the rules of the game for exporting to Europe or importing from Europe fundamentally change,' he noted, with the consequence that some 'very big' and 'highly profitable' industries would simply become 'uneconomic'. By 30 October, the National Institute of Economic and Social Research (NIESR) was reporting that even if the UK avoided a no-deal Brexit by accepting the withdrawal agreement that Boris Johnson negotiated, it could cost the UK economy more than £70bn over the course of the next 10 years.

However, while it is perhaps unsurprising that much of the discussion surrounding Brexit focused on the potential benefits of 'leaving' or 'remaining' in terms of the economy, or control over the UK's national borders, the fallout from the process is likely to have wider and more significant consequences for the nation's constitutional arrangements. While some might argue that *The Economist* overstated the case when describing Brexit as 'Britain's constitutional time-bomb' in its May 2019 leader column, the

2016 EU referendum has certainly put many long-established constitutional conventions under strain, and left the constitution as a whole in a considerable state of flux.

Whereas in Chapter 1 we focused on the question of whether citizens' assemblies might help elected politicians to chart a way through this constitutional minefield, this chapter focuses instead on the range and scale of challenges facing the UK constitution.

In doing so, it will consider the following issues:

- Why has Brexit been described as a 'constitutional time-bomb'?
- What does Brexit mean for the constitutional protection afforded to rights?
- What does Brexit mean for the union?
- What does Brexit mean for constitutional arrangements at Westminster?

## Why has Brexit been described as a 'constitutional time-bomb'?

In the absence of a codified constitution in the UK (see Boxes 5.1 and 5.2), the patchwork of rules that governs the relationships between the various institutions that comprise the state, and the relationship between the state and its citizens, has evolved over time through the passage of legislation and the emergence of conventions.

### Box 5.1 What is a constitution?

- A constitution is a body of laws, rules and practices that sets out the way in which a state or society is organised.
- A constitution establishes the relationship between the state and its citizens, and also between the various institutions that constitute the state.
- A constitution provides a framework for the political system, establishing the main institutions of government, determining where decision-making authority resides and protecting the basic rights of citizens, often in a formal bill of rights.

### Box 5.2 Codified and uncodified constitutions

- **Codified constitution:** a single authoritative document that sets out the laws, rules and principles by which a state is governed, and protects the rights of citizens.
- **Uncodified constitution:** where the laws, rules and principles specifying how a state is to be governed are not gathered in a single document. Instead they are found in a variety of sources, some written (e.g. statute law) and some unwritten (e.g. convention).

Since the UK joined the European Economic Community (EEC) on 1 January 1973, the various treaties and European institutions that it signed up to at that time, and the further European treaties and laws that have flowed from them, have become a key fifth source of such constitutional rules and regulations (see Box 5.3). The Treaty of Rome (1957), upon which the EEC was founded, was incorporated into UK law under the European Communities Act 1972, the piece of statute law that confirmed the UK's accession into the EEC. In accepting the Treaty of Rome, the UK Parliament agreed to accept the authority of European law over UK law where the two were in conflict, while also accepting the authority of the European Commission and the European Court of Justice to adjudicate in the case of disputes arising thereof.

**Box 5.3 Sources of the UK constitution in September 2019**

1. Statute law
2. Common law
3. Conventions
4. Authoritative works (or 'works of authority')
5. European Union laws and treaties

What this means, in short, is that leaving the EU removes what has become one of the pillars of the UK constitution over the course of the past 40 years – most notably in respect of the protection of individual rights and liberties. However, while such a change might be seen as delivering on the Leave campaign's promise to 'take back control' and restore national sovereignty, Brexit may also have other, more far-reaching implications for the UK's constitutional arrangements:

- Taking the UK as a whole out of the EU, when Scotland voted so overwhelmingly to remain, brings into question the very future of the union, as does the failure to arrive at a workable solution with regards to how to regulate the post-Brexit border between Northern Ireland and the Republic of Ireland without restoring a so-called 'hard border'.
- The assertiveness demonstrated by the House of Commons and its speaker in the face of Theresa May's efforts to gain approval for her withdrawal agreement, and again subsequently in the wake of Boris Johnson's efforts to prorogue parliament as a means of preventing the legislature from blocking a no-deal Brexit, also raises fundamental questions about the relationship between the executive, the legislature and the judiciary.

## What does Brexit mean for the constitutional protection afforded to human rights?

Some of the enthusiasm for 'taking back control' on the Leave side of the Brexit debate was fuelled by a sense that the European Courts were exercising undue control over the UK's own political and judicial institutions. This was particularly true in the area of human rights, where editorials in the more right-leaning newspapers were often seen to bemoan the fact that UK authorities were unable to deal with terrorist suspects in the face of judicial interference from Strasbourg.

It is true that membership of the European Union has clearly added a layer of additional protection and regulation to the rights enjoyed by EU citizens. Adherence to the Charter of Fundamental Rights (CFR) of the European Union, for example, is a key element of EU membership. Even when one places the CFR to one side, however, it is clear that a good deal of the UK's own equality legislation is based upon other EU laws and regulations. The government made a commitment as part of its post-Brexit planning to put in place measures to mirror the protections currently offered as part of EU membership. However, this is clearly only a short-term expedient to allow for smooth transition to life outside of the EU, with UK rights legislation likely to evolve along divergent pathways thereafter. In that sense, the protection afforded to human rights in the UK will inevitably change, to some degree at least, post-Brexit.

Ironically, however, much of the criticism of European judges is aimed not at the European Court of Justice, the 'Supreme Court' of the EU, but at the European Court of Human Rights (ECtHR). Although the latter is, somewhat confusingly, based in Strasbourg, a key centre of EU operations, the ECtHR is not an EU institution. It was instead established by the Council of Europe, the intergovernmental organisation that drafted the European Convention on Human Rights (ECHR) in 1950 (see Table 5.1). In truth, it is that convention, fully incorporated into UK law under the Human Rights Act (HRA) 1998, which has had a hand in many of the cases that have led to criticism from those on the right. Crucially, however, leaving the EU does not mean that the UK will leave the Council of Europe, reject the ECHR or repeal the HRA, or reject the authority of the ECtHR. Indeed, there is no suggestion that the government is even contemplating going down that road.

***Table 5.1 The European courts***

| The European Court of Human Rights (ECtHR) | The European Court of Justice (ECJ) |
|---|---|
| ■ Established by the Council of Europe<br>■ Hears cases brought under the ECHR<br>■ Based in Strasbourg but not an EU institution | ■ The 'Supreme Court' of the EU<br>■ Hears cases arising under EU law<br>■ Based in Luxembourg |

**Weblink:** 'What does Brexit mean for equality and human rights in the UK?', 20 July 2017: **www.equalityhumanrights.com**

## What does Brexit mean for the union?

### Scotland

Although the 2014 Scottish referendum was expected to settle the debate over independence for a generation or more, the relative closeness of that result, and the outcome of the Brexit referendum just 2 years later, means that IndyRef2 is still very much on the agenda. Although preserving the integrity of the United Kingdom was one strand of the 'No' campaign in the independence referendum, another equally strong argument in favour of remaining in the UK was what independence might mean for the nation's membership of the EU. As it was the UK, and not its constituent nations, which joined the EEC back in 1973, it was argued that a newly independent Scotland would not be an EU member state by right. Instead, Scotland would have to go through an application process that would be subject to veto by any member state and make the adjustments to the Scottish economy that are required in order to meet EU entry requirements. It was even suggested that Scotland, like any other new state joining the EU, would have to be prepared to adopt the euro.

Yet, while a desire to remain in the EU was a key factor in delivering the 'no' vote on Scottish independence, the fact that the UK as a whole voted to leave the EU just 2 years later (51.9% to 48.1%) while Scotland voted emphatically to remain (see Table 5.2) had the effect of reopening the independence debate. Crucially, many of those who had voted against independence were offered the possibility that IndyRef2 might be a means of keeping Scotland in the EU, or taking an independent Scotland back in even though the rest of the UK was leaving. The SNP performance in the 2019 EU elections only served to reinforce the sense that a second independence referendum could be on the cards, a fact that Labour Shadow Chancellor John McDonnell controversially acknowledged in comments he made publicly on 7 August.

***Table 5.2 Brexit results for the UK's nations***

| | England | Northern Ireland | Scotland | Wales |
|---|---|---|---|---|
| **Leave** | 53.4%<br>15,188,406 votes | 44.2%<br>349,442 votes | 38.0%<br>1,018,322 votes | 52.5%<br>854,572 votes |
| **Remain** | 46.6%<br>13,266,996 votes | 55.8%<br>440,707 votes | 62.0%<br>1,661,191 votes | 47.5%<br>772,347 votes |

## Northern Ireland

Scotland aside, the practicalities of Brexit in relation to the border between Northern Ireland and the Republic of Ireland could also be seen to threaten the union. Although this border could remain relatively free from controls while both the UK and the Republic of Ireland are within the UK, the EU as a single market would obviously not be able to countenance such a porous outer EU border once the UK departed. There would either need to be a physical, 'hard' border, or some other means of preventing the existing border being used as a back door into and out of the EU for goods and citizens. While the terms of the Northern Ireland peace settlement effectively made a hard border a non-starter, parliament roundly rejected the only acceptable alternative to the EU – the so-called 'backstop', agreed as part of Theresa May's EU withdrawal agreement. Although Boris Johnson's solution to the same problem, which effectively created a border in the Irish Sea, gained more support among Conservative Eurosceptics, it was roundly rejected by their DUP allies. In this context, and with devolved government in Northern Ireland effectively suspended since disagreements between the executive and the assembly back

in January 2017, some even speculated that the unification of the island of Ireland might be the only way beyond the impasse. Although such an outcome could be triggered by means of a so-called 'border poll', as provided for in the 1998 Northern Ireland Act, polling data would suggest that the wider public are not ready for such a move, in the north at least: an *Irish Times*/Ipsos MRBI poll found that just 38% of the Northern Ireland public thought there should be such a referendum on unification and only 32% said they would vote 'yes' in such a referendum, against the 45% who would vote 'no', or the 23% who 'don't know'.

## What does Brexit mean for constitutional arrangements at Westminster?

The parliamentary ping-pong surrounding Brexit has clearly been of constitutional significance for central government relations, irrespective of the path the UK takes once the impasse is resolved.

### 1 The relationship between the executive and the legislature

While governments lacking a workable Commons majority often face significant opposition in parliament, the extent to which the legislature asserted itself over the course of the Brexit negotiations was noteworthy. The ability of the Commons to seize control of parliamentary business and hold indicative votes on a range of possible outcomes, and the willingness of the speaker, John Bercow, to facilitate that process, was without recent precedent. That much was amply demonstrated both by Bercow's willingness to assert the authority of the chamber by blocking government attempts to bring Theresa May's EU withdrawal agreement back for a fourth vote and, later, by the part that he played in facilitating the introduction and passage of the so-called 'Benn Act' (see Box 5.4).

**Box 5.4 The European Union (Withdrawal) (No. 2) Act 2019 (the'Benn Act')**

- The Act was forced through the Commons in a day in the face of Boris Johnson's decision to prorogue parliament.
- It required the prime minister to send a letter by 19 October requesting a Brexit extension, unless the Commons had approved a withdrawal agreement or agreed to a no-deal Brexit by that date.
- It provided a draft of the letter that the prime minister should send, specified the length of extension that should be requested (to 31 January 2020), and obliged the prime minister to accept that extension, if offered.
- It required the government to publish a series of progress reports on Brexit negotiations that would include a report every 4 weeks from 7 February 2020.

### 2 A challenge to established conventions

The suggestion by leading government ministers that they might seek to prorogue parliament or call a general election as a means of stopping parliament from preventing a no-deal Brexit at the end of October – even though the Commons had already explicitly rejected such a no-deal Brexit – should also be seen as a watershed moment. Widely characterised by commentators on the left as a threat to suspend democracy, such a move was also a strange path to take for those Leave campaigners who championed parliamentary sovereignty during the 2016 referendum campaign. The possibility that an early vote of no confidence in Boris Johnson's administration might be used as a means of preventing such a course of action, and debates over whether or not Johnson would have to go in the event that he lost such a vote, also highlighted the vagaries of the UK constitution in such matters – with the imprecision and ambiguity of the Fixed-term Parliaments Act 2011 only serving to add a further level of uncertainty. The manner in which parliament was ultimately able to circumvent that Act and schedule a general election on 12 December 2019 only served to underline the point.

### 3 A question mark over the role of the House of Lords and the monarch

At a time of such political controversy, and in the wake of a clear if not crushing victory for the Leave campaign in the 2016 referendum, attention has again turned to the House of Lords and the question of whether it is right that an unelected chamber should retain the ability to frustrate the ambitions of elected politicians. Faced with such a fast-moving landscape, where governments are driven less by their stated manifesto commitments and more by the shifting sands of political necessity, the Salisbury convention (see Box 5.5) seems both anachronistic and all too easily set aside. By November 2019, the government's ever-shrinking Commons majority, the extent to which the Brexit proposition had changed beyond all recognition since the referendum and the mid-term change in prime minister had all served to strengthen the House of Lords' hand. The constitutional position of the monarch was also under discussion – particularly when in the event of a vote of no confidence in Boris Johnson's government, and his refusal to go quietly or his desire to call an election that would have seen Brexit occur by default while parliament was suspended, the monarch would most likely have had to 'make the call' on what should happen.

#### Box 5.5 The Salisbury Doctrine

Dating from 1945, the Salisbury Doctrine established the convention that the Lords – as an unelected chamber – should not oppose government bills at second reading where the government had established a clear electoral mandate to act by including a measure in its manifesto.

### 4 The evolution of the UK Supreme Court

The willingness of the Supreme Court to step in and hear cases arising from Boris Johnson's decision to prorogue parliament, and the ruling that the court handed down in that case (see Box 5.6), marked a significant watershed in the evolution of that institution. Although the creation of the court under the Constitutional Reform Act 2005 was portrayed as being more about enhancing the separation of powers than about enhancing the power and jurisdiction of the highest court in the land, there was always the suspicion that things might take on a life of their own in the years that followed, as we noted in the *2006 Annual Survey*, 3 years before the court opened for business (see Box 5.7).

### Box 5.6 The UK Supreme Court's prorogation ruling (24 September 2019)

- The court argued that the use of the royal prerogative, in this case to prorogue parliament, must always respect the conventions of parliamentary sovereignty and democratic accountability.
- Any prorogation that had 'the effect of frustrating or preventing, without reasonable justification, the ability of parliament to carry out its constitutional functions as a legislature' would be unlawful.
- The prorogation in question had an 'extreme' effect on the 'fundamentals of democracy', coming as it did at such a crucial point in the Brexit process.
- The court declared the prorogation unlawful and quashed the relevant Order in Council. This meant that parliament had, in law, never been prorogued, so MPs were free to return. As president of the Supreme Court, Baroness Hale, stated: 'The Court is bound to conclude that the decision to advise Her Majesty to prorogue Parliament was unlawful because it had the effect of frustrating or preventing the ability of Parliament to carry out its constitutional functions without reasonable justification.'

### Box 5.7 Predictions for the UK Supreme Court

As has been the case with the Human Rights Act 1998 and the Freedom of Information Act 2000, it is likely that the new Supreme Court will take time to establish itself in the public consciousness. The relationship between the court, the public, the government and parliament will also take time to formalise. In this respect, the UK Supreme Court may have more in common with its US counterpart than one would initially think. After all, the latter's power of judicial review was not set out explicitly in Article III of the constitution, but discovered by the court itself in cases such as Marbury v. Madison (1803). It may be that the new UK Supreme Court will have to carve out a role for itself in a similar way.

**Source:** Fairclough, P., Kelly, R., Magee, E. (2006) *UK Government and Politics Annual Survey*, Philip Allan

## Conclusion

Although the debate surrounding Brexit has often been framed in economic terms, or in relation to border control, it has had major political and constitutional implications for three key reasons:

1 In the absence of a codified constitution, EU treaties, laws and regulations have come to fill in a lot of the gaps in respect of the protection of rights and individual liberties.

2 It is argued that Brexit has the potential to result in the unravelling of the United Kingdom.

3 It has unsettled the long-established relationships between the main actors and institutions that lie at the heart of Westminster politics.

Quite how the UK will resolve such complex and, in some cases, apparently insoluble problems in the wake of its departure from the EU is uncertain. What is clear, however, is that Brexit was, first, always going to be a good deal more complex than some of the prime movers in the Leave campaign sought to make out and, second, it will have an impact that is significantly wider and more lasting in constitutional terms than even many 'remainers' warned.

### Summary

- Although Brexit has major economic implications for the UK it also has an impact on a range of other aspects of UK politics, many of them constitutional.
- Membership of the EU has contributed to the development of a rights culture in the UK, and the extent and manner in which rights are protected post-Brexit will inevitably be subject to change.
- The overwhelming rejection of Brexit by Scottish voters at the 2016 referendum has fuelled calls for a further referendum on Scottish independence (IndyRef2). This presents a significant challenge to the future of the UK, as does the question of how to manage the border between Northern Ireland and the Republic of Ireland in the wake of Brexit.
- Arguments over Brexit have placed the relationship between the government and parliament under significant pressure, bringing a number of long-established conventions into question.
- Such developments meant that the monarch, long-regarded as a 'dignified' (i.e. largely symbolic and ceremonial) element of the UK constitution, might have been called upon to make key decisions.
- Boris Johnson's decision to prorogue parliament, and the unusual length of that prorogation, saw the UK Supreme Court breaking new ground:
  - first, by deciding that it had the right to review the use of a prerogative power
  - second, by ruling the prime minister's prorogation unlawful and void

### How can I use this information in my exam?

Brexit can feature in your exam answers across a range of different topics and units — whether it be in relation to the role of specific institutions, such as the House of Lords, the nature of the UK's decision to leave the EU in and of itself, or in analysing the UK's evolving constitutional arrangements. The constitutional impact of Brexit is likely to be especially significant, and highlights many of the idiosyncrasies of the British constitutional system. One of the key considerations when including Brexit in your answers is to ensure that the information you use is as up-to-date and relevant as possible, especially given the rapidly changing situation.

## Consolidation activities

1. What is a constitution and what different types of constitution exist?
2. How has UK membership of the EU affected the UK constitution?
3. How and why might the UK leaving the EU change the relationship between Scotland and England?
4. Outline some of the ways in which the protection of individual rights would both change and stay the same in the wake of Brexit.
5. Explain the ways in which the actions of the speaker of the House of Commons and the actions of the UK Supreme Court were important in relation to the Brexit process in 2019.
6. What, in your opinion, will prove to be the most significant constitutional development resulting from the Brexit process? Provide evidence to support your assertion.

hapter 6

# Education policy in Scotland: holding the government to account

## Exam success

The up-to-date facts, examples and arguments in this chapter will help you to produce good-quality answers in the following specification areas:

| N5 Modern Studies | Higher Modern Studies | Higher Politics |
|---|---|---|
| • Power and decision making (Scotland)<br>• Participation (Scotland)<br>• Representation (Scotland) | • Effectiveness of parliamentary representatives in holding the government to account<br>• Ways in which citizens can influence decision making | • Political parties and elections — the dominant ideas within political parties<br>• Political systems — the legislative branch; the executive branch |

## Context

One of the long-standing focuses of the Scottish government has been the field of education policy. Specifically, there have been several initiatives and drives to close the so-called 'attainment gap', the difference between the performance of pupils from different social and economic backgrounds at school. Many children and young people living in Scotland's most deprived areas perform significantly worse at school than those from less deprived areas, and it has been a much-touted aim of the SNP government to close this gap. Education is seen as a key tool in reducing social inequality, because it enables young people to access a wider range of career and further education options after they leave school, and therefore creates a more equal and fairer society.

In examining Scottish educational policies, we will look at some of the initiatives and policies introduced by the SNP government in Scotland in order to close the attainment gap. This chapter will then go on to briefly evaluate the effectiveness of these policies. It will also focus on the effectiveness of parliamentary representatives in holding the government to account in this area, as well as showing how citizens can influence decision making more generally.

In doing so, this chapter will consider the following issues:

- What is the 'attainment gap'?
- What actions is the SNP government taking to 'close the gap'?
- How can the Scottish government be held accountable?

## What is the 'attainment gap'?

A high-quality education provided for all has long been seen as one of the principal ways to create a more equal society. John Swinney MSP, the deputy first minister and cabinet secretary for education and skills, recently pointed out in the report 'Education governance – next steps' that improving the education and life chances of children and young people in Scotland is the defining mission of the SNP government.

Yet, there is clear evidence that the gap in the attainment between pupils from the richest and poorest households in Scotland persists, and that this gap starts in preschool years and continues throughout primary and secondary school. What is also clear is that in most cases this gap widens throughout a young person's school career, impacting individual's post-school options and income levels in adulthood.

### What evidence is there that an attainment gap exists?

Several studies have been undertaken into educational inequality. The Scottish Survey of Literacy and Numeracy, for example, monitors academic attainment at key stages of primary and secondary school from Primary 4 to S2. Its most recent report, in 2016, identified several indicators suggesting that Scotland had an attainment gap (see Box 6.1). Put simply, the proportion of pupils who performed well or very well increased as they became less deprived across all stages of education – and this gap in attainment appears to be widening, rather than closing.

**Box 6.1** **Attainment by deprivation, Scottish Survey of Literacy and Numeracy (2016)**

- The percentage of pupils performing well or very well in reading in Primary 4 was 67% for the most deprived, and 85% for the least deprived.
- The percentage of pupils performing well or very well in reading in S2 was 73% for the most deprived, and 89% for the least deprived.
- Those from the most deprived backgrounds performed less well in 2016 than in 2012.
- Those from the least deprived backgrounds performed just as well in 2016 as they did in 2012.

### What problems result from an inequality gap?

According to the Joseph Rowntree Foundation, over 1 in 5 children live in poverty in Scotland today, and this affects their health, education and future work prospects. Although arguably Scottish education is effective for many children, there is an argument that it does not serve the most vulnerable, and that the gap in educational attainment between pupils from the richest and poorest backgrounds is wider than in similar countries. The Organisation for Economic Co-operation and Development (OECD) made this argument in a report into education in Scotland (see Box 6.2).

**Box 6.2 'Quality and Equity of Schooling in Scotland' (OECD review, 2007)**

'Little of the variation in the student achievement in Scotland is associated with the ways in which schools differ... Who you are in Scotland is far more important than what school you attend, so far as achievement differences on international tests are concerned. Socioeconomic status is the most important difference between individuals.'

The argument the OECD presented is that if you come from a poorer background, you are likely to do less well in school, and therefore have fewer options in later life than those from wealthier backgrounds attending a similar school.

## What actions is the SNP government taking to 'close the gap'?

The SNP government has been active in developing and reforming education policy with the aim of delivering a high quality education for all young people in Scotland, therefore affording all young people with the options to pursue higher and further education, or to enter the workplace.

One way in which the Scottish government is trying to improve education is through the Attainment Scotland Fund (ASF). This is a targeted initiative focused on closing the attainment gap between the most and least disadvantaged children. The ASF has identified several Challenge Authorities (see Box 6.3) where there has been a focus on improving literacy, numeracy, and health and well-being.

**Box 6.3 Attainment Scotland Fund Challenge Authorities**

- Glasgow
- Dundee
- Clackmannanshire
- North Lanarkshire
- East Ayrshire
- Renfrewshire

The Attainment Scotland Fund distributes around £750 million in such a way as to support the pupils from the most deprived areas, and with a heavy focus on primary schools. The money is distributed across Scottish schools based on the needs identified by local authorities, headteachers, and chief social work and education officers.

### Are the government responses to education inequality effective?

There have been some reports that this focus combined with financial resources can have, and is having, a positive impact on improving education and narrowing the attainment gap. Renfrewshire has received £10.4 million in Scottish government Attainment Challenge funding since June 2016, and was the first area to be rated 'excellent' for its progress in improving learning, with the poverty related attainment gap reducing by 6% in literacy and 4% in numeracy.

**Weblink:** 'Renfrewshire Council's progress on narrowing the attainment gap praised', BBC News, 19 February 2019: **www.bbc.co.uk**

Additionally, the deputy first minister pointed out the continuing success of the Scottish education system more broadly in closing the attainment gap, arguing that Scotland's education system is delivering improving results. In 'Scotland's education reform: update', published June 2018, he highlighted that 23% of school leavers from the most deprived areas now attend university, compared with 16.5% from 7 years ago. Additionally, the interim evaluation of the Attainment Scotland Fund showed that 78% of teachers had already seen an improvement in attainment and well-being as a result of the fund, and 97% of headteachers expected to see further improvements in the coming 5 years. This suggests that the ASF is effective in targeting those young people who need the greatest support, and that it is helping young people from the most deprived areas get into university and work, giving them greater opportunity in the future.

However, there have been others who argue that the government response to closing the attainment gap has been less effective. The Scottish Conservative Party has argued that there has been a 0.1% increase in students from the most deprived areas getting a university place in 2019, and there has likewise been an increase of 0.7% of young people from the most affluent areas going to university, suggesting that the attainment gap is in fact widening (see Box 6.4). This suggests that although pupils from poorer backgrounds are performing better at school, they are not improving as significantly as pupils from the least deprived areas.

### Box 6.4 Statement from the Conservative education spokeswoman Liz Smith MSP

> The gap between the most and least well-off students has risen and it is utterly misleading of the SNP government to claim otherwise.

**Weblink:** 'Row over Scottish ministers' education gap claims' by Scott Macnab, 9 August 2019: **www.scotsman.com/education**

These conflicting interpretations have been the focus of much of the business in parliament, especially given that the first minister had outlined education as the highest priority.

## How can the Scottish government be held accountable?

Clearly there is a debate about how successful the Scottish government is in delivering an improvement to Scottish education. However, how can it be held accountable for its progress in this area? In common with most other liberal democracies, there are a number of ways in which the Scottish government can be held to account in areas such as education policy (see Box 6.5).

## Box 6.5 Ways the Scottish government can be held accountable

- The first minister and their cabinet are collectively accountable to the Scottish Parliament for their policies and actions.
- They are expected to appear before parliament each week to answer questions from MSPs.
- Political parties are accountable to voters in elections, and voters can select both their local and regional representatives.
- Committees play a role in scrutinising the government and, in the absence of an 'upper house', have significant power.
- The Public Petitions Committee considers any issues raised by members of the public and brought to parliament by petition.

### Role of committees in holding the government to account

One of the main roles of committees in the Scottish Parliament is to hold the government to account. Committees reflect the balance of parties across parliament, and can be either mandatory or subject committees. Mandatory committees are set down under the Scottish Parliament's standing orders, and include the Equalities and Human Rights Committee and the Finance and Constitution Committee. Subject committees are set up at the beginning of each parliamentary session, and they usually correspond with a specific government department. For example, the Education and Skills Committee scrutinises the government's performance in relation to policies connected to education. It consists of 11 MSPs from five political parties.

Committees have the power to question government policy, or to ask for clarification of findings or evidence. For example, after the 2018 exam results were published, the Education and Skills Committee heard evidence from academics, teachers and also representatives from the Scottish Qualifications Authority (SQA). Its members wrote to John Swinney MSP, the cabinet secretary for education and skills, and asked for his perspective on the evidence that had been presented, as well as if the government was planning any relevant work in that area. The convenor of the committee also has the power to ask for a response by a certain date, ensuring that the government cannot avoid feeding back to committees. The letters, minutes and proceedings of these committee hearings are open and transparent, and can be viewed via the Scottish government's website.

The committee was especially active in hearing evidence on the issue of attainment of school-aged children experiencing poverty, and it held five formal meetings and had 104 official submissions on the matter in 2018.

**Weblink:** Education and Skills Committee meeting, 6 February 2019: **www.scottishparliament.tv**

### Role of petitions in holding the government to account

Committees are not the only way in which the government may be held accountable. One way in which citizens can become involved in challenging government policy is to sign a petition. Petitions are a formal written request to the government requesting that an action is taken in a specific matter. For example, a petition in August 2019 (PE01747: Adequate funding to support children with additional support need in all Scottish Schools) called for more money to be made available in order for mainstream primary and secondary schools to support pupils with additional support needs. Once certain criteria are met, the Public Petitions Committee may consider the issues raised and the matter is heard in parliament. This allows citizens a more direct way of participating in democracy in Scotland.

### Role of MSPs in holding the government to account

MSPs have the opportunity to ask the first minister questions during First Minister's Questions every Thursday, or to participate in parliamentary debates. This provides MSPs with the opportunity to challenge the government on issues such as education. For example, on 15 May 2019, Tavish Scott (Liberal Democrat) used parliamentary debate to challenge the effectiveness of the government's education policy. He proposed a motion that although the SNP had outlined that education was the number one government priority, its actions had not reflected this. The deputy first minister had the opportunity to respond, and other MSPs added comments or questions. This system allows MSPs to constantly critique the government's actions, and the effectiveness of their policies, such as in this case of education policy. This provides us with a clear example of how the legislative branch can hold the executive to account.

**Weblink:** Scottish parliamentary business, motions, questions and answers: **www.parliament.scot/parliamentarybusiness.aspx**

### Summary

- The SNP has championed educational reform as a government priority, with a major focus within that of reducing inequality in education.
- It has invested significant resources and time in reducing the attainment gap between the most and least deprived young people.
- The government is held accountable in areas such as educational policy via committees, which have significant powers.
- Citizens can participate in holding the government to account via petitions.
- The first minister and their cabinet are accountable to MSPs via established practices such as First Minister's Questions and parliamentary debate.

## How can I use this information in my exam?

Although educational inequality is an issue worthy of consideration on its own merits, the fact that the first minister and the deputy first minister have identified education as a 'number one priority' for the SNP government provides a second level of interest for students of Modern Studies and Politics.

What this focus-piece on education also reveals is that the Scottish Parliament has several methods of holding the government to account in relation to its efforts to make improvements in Scottish education. Committees, petitions, debates and questions all allow citizens and parliamentary representatives to challenge the government and hold it accountable. Motions, such as the one proposed by Tavish Scott, show that MSPs can directly challenge the actions of government. Case studies such as this can also be used to demonstrate how the legislative branch can hold the executive branch accountable in a wider sense.

## Consolidation activities

1. What evidence is there of an 'attainment gap' in Scotland?
2. What policies has the SNP government in Scotland introduced to close this gap?
3. How effective have the government's actions been? Make a table or a series of bullet-point lists that categorise the available evidence under the following headings:

| Effective | Less effective | Ineffective |
|---|---|---|
| | | |

4. Produce an illustrated spider diagram detailing the ways in which the Scottish government can be held to account. Add as much detail as possible.
5. In your opinion, which is the most effective way of holding the government to account? Provide evidence in support of your choice.

# Chapter 7

# Scottish independence: is it getting closer, and what would it look like?

## Exam success

The up-to-date facts, examples and arguments in this chapter will help you to produce good-quality answers in the following specification areas:

| Nat 5 Modern Studies | Higher Modern Studies | Higher Politics |
|---|---|---|
| • Power and decision making (Scotland/UK)<br>• Participation (Scotland) | • Possible alternatives to the governance of Scotland | • Political theory — power, authority and legitimacy |

## Context

The 2014 Scottish independence referendum, labelled a 'once in a generation event', saw the 'No' campaign win, with a clear majority of 55% to 45% of the Scottish people wishing to remain as part of the United Kingdom. However, just 5 years later, the first minister tabled a bill to put the question of Scottish independence to the Scottish people once again.

There has been much debate about whether or not it is valid to ask Scots to vote on independence again and so soon after the last referendum. Proponents of such a move point to a significantly different political climate: most obviously, perhaps, the fact that while 62% of Scots voted to remain in the EU, the likelihood of a 'no deal' Brexit increased significantly over the course of 2019. The selection of Boris Johnson as Conservative leader, and therefore prime minister, and his party's subsequent victory in the 2019 general election have arguably also boosted the case for an independent Scotland, given his apparent unpopularity north of the border. Put simply, a combination of Brexit uncertainty and an unpopular Westminster Conservative government has seemingly undermined general support for the union, with former prime minister Gordon Brown remarking that we now live in 'at best, only a precariously United Kingdom'.

Scotland cannot hold another referendum without legislation being passed in Westminster, something that the previous prime minister, Theresa May, said she would not permit. Johnson has also stated publicly that he views the question of independence as one that has been answered, for the time being at least. This position naturally puts the government of Westminster at odds with the SNP government in Scotland, who can easily point to the highest polling rates since 2016 in favour of independence.

This chapter will therefore consider the following issues:

- What factors make Scottish independence more likely?
- What factors make Scottish independence less likely?
- What do the opinion polls show?
- What might an independent Scotland look like?

## What factors make Scottish independence more likely?

In the wake of the 2011 Scottish election, the SNP secured, for the first time, a parliamentary majority to push for the first independence referendum. The former first minister Alex Salmond and former prime minister David Cameron agreed that the Scottish people should be asked whether or not Scotland should be an independent country, and in 2014 Scots voted to remain in the United Kingdom. This referendum had been called a 'once in a generation event', yet recent calls for another independence referendum (IndyRef2) have been advanced by some in Scotland, led by the first minister Nicola Sturgeon. Why has the issue come to the fore once again and what factors make independence more likely?

### 1 Scotland voting 'remain' in the 2016 EU referendum

There was a stark contrast between how Scotland answered the referendum on EU membership and how voters balloted elsewhere in the UK. While a clear majority of voters in England and Wales voted to leave the EU, 62% of Scots voted to remain in a campaign focused firmly on the importance of the EU for the Scottish economy. Such an apparent mismatch only served to reinforce the sense that, in spite of devolution, a Scotland that remained within the union left the government in Westminster with the power to drag the country in a direction that is diametrically opposed to the wishes of Scots. The SNP uses this as evidence to argue that there is a democratic deficit in the UK, and that with such political divergence it is increasingly logical for Scotland to become independent. This argument has been especially powerful when linked to a possible decision to leave the EU without a deal. A recent 'HOPE not hate' poll showed that 60% of Scots felt that support for independence would increase if the UK left the EU without a deal, with only 14% of Scots polled believing that leaving the EU without a deal was a good idea.

### 2 EU elections

Scotland's overwhelming desire to remain in the EU despite the wishes of the rest of the UK was reflected in the results of the 2019 EU elections. Nicola Sturgeon famously called for all Scots, even those against independence, to support the SNP in sending a resounding message that Scots did not want Brexit. This clear anti-Brexit message contributed to the SNP's electoral success, while the party returned the largest number of Scottish MEPs to Brussels and increased its vote from 29% in 2014 to 37.7% in 2019. The first minister said that this result shows that '[Scotland] will not accept a Brexit process that... fails to represent the interests of the people of Scotland'. The results in Scotland with significant gains

for remain parties like the SNP and Liberal Democrats, contrasted with the gains made by the Brexit Party (29 MEPs and 31.6% share of the vote) south of the border (see Table 7.1).

***Table 7.1 The Scottish parties' share of the vote in the 2019 EU elections***

| Party | SNP | Labour | Liberal Democrat | Conservative | Green | Brexit |
|---|---|---|---|---|---|---|
| **Share of the vote** | 37.7% | 9.3% | 13.9% | 11.6% | 8.2% | 14.8% |
| **Change in share of the vote** | +8.7% | –16.6% | +6.8% | –5.6% | 0.1% | N/A |

### 3 Labour's position on Scottish independence

When the Labour shadow chancellor, John McDonnell, visited Scotland in August 2019 for the Edinburgh Festival, he made the announcement that if elected, Labour would not stand in the way of another Scottish referendum. This shocked many, most notably the leader of the Scottish Labour Party, Richard Leonard, because it appeared to signal an important shift in Labour policy. Jeremy Corbyn later confirmed that while he was against the break-up of the UK, it was not Westminster's place to block another referendum. While some have argued that this may have been a way for Corbyn to galvanise opposition support in parliament, it nevertheless appeared to remove much of the opposition to IndyRef2.

### 4 How Scotland voted at GE2019

The SNP's strong performance at the 2019 general election could also be said to have strengthened their mandate for a second referendum (see p. 26).

## What factors make Scottish independence less likely?

Despite growing calls for another independence referendum from pro-independence supporters and politicians, there remain significant hurdles to achieving IndyRef2. Such barriers stem primarily from the constitutional arrangements laid out in the Scotland Act 1998, which states that all issues concerning the union are reserved to Westminster.

### The Scotland Act 1998

The Scottish government, although tabling legislation to allow another referendum to take place, has made clear that it wishes to proceed with a legal referendum, fearing that otherwise the Supreme Court may block any result or debar Scotland's entry into the EU at a later date. This means that, constitutionally speaking, Westminster must grant Scotland permission to hold any referendum that pertains to the union. In April 2019, then prime minister Theresa May resisted calls for IndyRef2, arguing first that the question was answered in 2014, and second that this 'was a time for the UK to pull together' in the face of Brexit. In September, the new prime minister, Boris Johnson – always a vocal supporter of the union – also spoke out in opposition to IndyRef2. While Johnson's willingness to consider constitutional reform in respect of the House of Lords and devolution to the English regions suggests that there might be at least a glimmer of hope for nationalists, there would appear to be little prospect of anything happening quickly without a change of government. Moreover, even if there were to be a second independence referendum, Westminster would remain in control of key details, such as the wording and timing of any public vote, in such a way as to make a 'yes' outcome less likely (see Box 7.1).

**Box 7.1 The Scotland Act 1998, Schedule 5, Reserved Matters**

The following aspects of the constitution are reserved matters, that is:

- **(a)** the Crown, including succession to the Crown and a regency
- **(b)** the Union of the Kingdoms of Scotland and England
- **(c)** the Parliament of the United Kingdom
- **(d)** the continued existence of the High Court of Justiciary as a criminal court of first instance and of appeal
- **(e)** the continued existence of the Court of Session as a civil court of first instance and of appeal

## What do the opinion polls show?

Recent polls have shown a slight increase of those in favour of Scottish independence. Indeed, in August 2019 a poll conducted by Lord Ashcroft (see Box 7.2) showed that there was even a narrow majority in favour – the first lead for independence since the Ipsos MORI survey of March 2017. Other polling conducted in the same month suggested that 47% of Scots felt that there should be another referendum on independence within the next 2 years, with 45% disagreeing. Significantly, while an overwhelming majority of those identifying as Conservative voters opposed another referendum, more than a third of Labour voters, more than half of EU Remain voters and even one in five of those who voted 'no' back in 2014 felt another referendum was appropriate. This suggests a growing public desire for IndyRef2.

**Box 7.2 Findings from Lord Ashcroft poll**

- A majority of Scots thought that if a second referendum were to be held, the result would be an independent Scotland.
- More than 6 in 10 Scots said they felt Brexit would make Scottish independence more likely.
- A slight majority of Scots (52%) said Brexit strengthens the case for Scotland to become independent.
- When Scots were asked to say whether it was more important for Scotland to be in the UK or the EU, 45% said in the EU and 43% said in the UK.

- When measuring how positively Scots felt about political leaders, Nicola Sturgeon had the highest approval rating.

**Weblink:** 'My Scotland poll: Yes to independence takes the lead', 5 August 2019: **https://lordashcroftpolls.com**

## What might an independent Scotland look like?

There is no certainty as to what an independent Scotland might look like, and although the government published a vision for independence in 2014, it is likely that this vision will continue to be modified. One area in which this has been especially clear is in currency, with a new currency strategy for an independent Scotland being developed at a recent SNP conference. Scotland would likely be a nation with a small armed force and no nuclear deterrent, and it would seek to join international institutions such as the UN and the EU as quickly as possible. This has been clarified in the SNP slogan 'an independent Scotland in an interdependent world'. However, what might key areas of an independent Scotland look like?

**Weblink:** Scotland's Future: **www2.gov.scot/resource/0043/00439021.pdf**

### 1 Currency

The case Alex Salmond and the Scottish government made in 2014 was to seek a currency union with England, which would see Scotland retaining the British pound in a trade-off for some economic freedoms. This was against the backdrop of a strong pound, particularly in relation to the euro. However, the chancellor of the exchequer at that time, George Osborne, rejected the plan, stating that if Scotland left the union it would also lose the pound. Recently the political and economic situation has changed, with a relatively weak pound and the likely economic impact of Brexit. This has led the SNP to call for the implementation of a new Scottish currency near the end of the first sitting government in an independent Scotland 'as soon as practicable'. Keith Brown MSP, deputy leader of the SNP, claimed that this 'provided a clear platform on which to campaign and win the case for independence', as it would leave Scotland free of economic controls south of the border. Interestingly, the SNP leader in Westminster, Ian Blackford, has consistently maintained that an independent Scotland would not necessarily be forced (or seek) to join the euro.

### 2 EU membership

Much of the government's planning hinges on gaining membership to the EU, which many argue is crucial to Scotland's economic success. This will likely be a complex process, though many Scottish politicians, including the first minister, have engaged as much as possible with European counterparts in order to secure goodwill. Some of this interaction has appeared to have been successful, with a former president of the EU, Herman Van Rompuy, stating that the EU would 'very seriously' consider Scottish membership, although he also cautioned that it would not be automatic. Van Rompuy also pointed out the difference between

Catalonia seeking independence and Scotland seeking to legally leave the UK and then apply for EU membership, highlighting that even the Spanish might not block Scotland's entry. However, as with the complex Brexit negotiations, nothing is certain until negotiations go live, which may be quite some time after an independence referendum.

## Conclusion

It is clear that the question of Scottish independence has come back to the fore, both in Scotland and in the UK more broadly. The impact of Brexit, the potential of a no deal and the general lack of popularity of the Johnson government have reignited the calls for independence. The increase in support for both IndyRef2 and Scottish independence has been significant, and could be said to add legitimacy to the first minister's call for another referendum. That being said, it is also likely that, as in other recent referendums, the referendum question would once again be divisive, with important questions about what an independent Scotland would look like also remaining.

Placing such reservations aside, it is significant that a second independence is being discussed seriously just 5 years after what was billed as a 'once in a generation event'. The fact that according to one poll the majority of Scots see such a course of action as both legitimate and desirable is all the more remarkable.

### Summary

- The Scottish government tabled a bill in April 2019 calling for legislation to bring about another independence referendum (IndyRef2).
- The democratic desires of Scotland have been at odds with those of England, as highlighted by the overwhelming vote to remain in the EU and the SNP's strong performance in EU elections and the 2019 general election.
- Polling in August 2019 showed a narrow majority of Scots supporting both IndyRef2 and Scottish independence.
- Scotland cannot hold another referendum without consent from Westminster — and that is unlikely to be forthcoming.
- Although the SNP is still developing its vision of what an independent Scotland might 'look like', it appears to involve joining the EU and adopting a new currency as soon as is practically possible.

### How can I use this information in my exam?

Information in this section relates directly to power and decision making in Scotland, and can be used to demonstrate how Scots are involved in determining their own futures. Additionally, comments can be made about the possible future relationship between Scotland, the UK and the EU, be it the impact of leaving the EU or alternatives for the governance of Scotland.

## Consolidation activities

1. Draw up a simple table which summarises the factors that make a second referendum 'more likely' or 'less likely'.
2. Explain, in detail, the factors that may make a second independence referendum more likely.
3. Explain, in detail, the factors that may make a second independence referendum less likely.
4. Identify which of the factors you find to be the most convincing and explain the reasons for your selections.
5. Explain, in detail, how the fallout from the 2016 EU referendum has influenced the developing debate over whether or not there should be a second independence referendum in Scotland.

hapter 8

# The 2019 general election: why did it happen and what did it tell us?

**Exam success**

The up-to-date facts, examples and arguments in this chapter will help you to produce good-quality answers in the following specification areas:

| NAT5 Modern Studies | Higher Modern Studies | Higher Politics |
|---|---|---|
| • Elections and campaigning (Scotland and UK)<br>• Voting systems | • Implications of the UK's decision to leave the European Union<br>• Strengths and weaknesses of different electoral systems used in elections within the UK<br>• Factors which influence voting behaviour including class, age and media | • The nature of democracy and different forms of democracy<br>• The impact of political campaign management strategies<br>• Theories of voting behaviour |

## Context

On 12 December 2019, voters went to the polls to cast their ballots in the third UK general election to be held in under 5 years. Such an eventuality would have appeared almost unthinkable just 8 years earlier, when the Fixed-term Parliaments Act theoretically set the interval between such contests to 5 years, in all but the most exceptional of circumstances. However, with both a parliament and a nation divided by Brexit, and a minority Conservative government giving full meaning to the oft-used expression 'in office, but not in power', all parties ultimately surrendered to the inevitable and voted through the Early Parliamentary General Election Act 2019, thereby circumventing the 2011 Act and allowing for the December poll.

This chapter offers a brief overview of the reasons why the 2019 general election was called and considers the efficacy of the means employed to achieve that goal, before moving on to consider the campaign itself and offer some tentative thoughts regarding its outcomes.

In doing so, it will consider the following questions:

- Why was there a general election in December 2019?
- Why was the 2019 general election campaign so unusual?
- Why did Labour lose?
- What can we learn from the 2019 general election?

## Why was there a general election in December 2019?

### Why did the Conservative government seek to call a general election in 2019?

In much the same way as Theresa May had failed on a number of occasions to secure parliamentary support for the Brexit withdrawal agreement she had negotiated with EU leaders, so Boris Johnson struggled to get his own deal across the line. In the event, the EU granted the Brexit extension that the prime minister had been forced to request under the terms of the 'Benn Act' (see Chapter 5), and parliament became deadlocked. Although Johnson had succeeded in getting his withdrawal agreement over its first parliamentary hurdle, the government knew that the agreement would be buried in multiple amendments were they to proceed. Similarly, whilst the Queen's Speech had also secured the backing of parliament, there appeared to be little appetite for returning to regular legislation while Brexit was still unresolved.

Against this backdrop, the government tried, but failed, to get the two-thirds Commons majority required to trigger an early general election under the Fixed-term Parliaments Act 2011. Although some of the other opposition parties, most notably the SNP, were keen to go to the polls, the Labour Party, under Jeremy Corbyn, had been reluctant to acquiesce until a no-deal Brexit had been taken off the table. Once the January extension had been agreed, that position became less tenable, with the Labour leader facing the accusation that he was running away from a general election in the knowledge that Labour would fare badly with him at the helm.

### Why did the means of securing the 2019 general election provoke controversy?

Ahead of the third and final effort to secure an early election under the Fixed-term Parliaments Act, on 28 October, some had suggested that the government might ultimately seek to circumvent that legislation by passing a one-line bill that explicitly scheduled an election on a predetermined date. However, many of those who favoured Brexit feared that such a bill could be amended to lower the voting age to 16 or extend the franchise to EU nationals – both of which might result in the election of a parliament that was less sympathetic to their cause.

With the Liberal Democrats and the SNP suggesting that they might themselves proffer such a bill, however, the government ultimately went ahead and tabled one of its own. That bill, which ultimately became the Early Parliamentary General Election Act 2019, set 12 December as the date of the next UK general election. It completed its passage through the Commons on 29 October, passed the Lords on 30 October and received Royal Assent on 31 October. With the Labour Party ultimately deciding to drop its opposition and support calls for an early poll, the Act ironically passed the Commons with the support of 438 MPs, a number greater than that which would have been required to call an election under the Fixed-term Parliaments Act.

While the scale of the Commons vote in favour of the new Act took some of the sting out of the debate, many nonetheless felt that there was something rather unseemly in the way parliament had looked to circumvent the Fixed-term Parliaments Act and deliver the government the general election it wanted, when it was parliament itself, during the time of the Coalition, that had sought to remove the right to decide the timing of general elections from the executive in order to prevent a government from scheduling such a democratic event to its political advantage.

## Why was the 2019 general election campaign so unusual?

Although the 2019 general election operated along the same lines and under the same electoral system that had been in place previously, there was a sense that it was a contest unlike any other in living memory. For many, the election was always going to be little more than a second Brexit referendum by proxy, with Boris Johnson campaigning to 'Get Brexit done' and most opposition parties offering further delay, followed by a second, actual referendum in order to confirm the outcome of the one held back in 2016.

The contest was further complicated by the position the SNP adopted, with the party campaigning on a ticket of rejecting Boris Johnson, stopping Brexit and giving the people of Scotland the right to decide whether or not to separate themselves from the UK. In Northern Ireland also, those nationalist parties who opposed Brexit, and favoured a border poll on a united Ireland, also looked to profit from disquiet over both Westminster's broad approach and also the specifics of the prime minister's withdrawal agreement as they related to trade between the British mainland and the island of Ireland.

Such existential threats to the union were mirrored by a similar state of flux in British party politics, with 18 MPs who had been returned to parliament back in 2017 either seeking election as independents or wearing the colours of a different party – whether having defected from one of the two main parties by choice, or having been forced out as a result of the whip being withdrawn.

The accepted wisdom in the face of such realities was that this would be an election in which traditional party ties would melt into the background and tactical voting would be absolutely key. While the latter did not ultimately materialise, the former was certainly evidenced in some of the polling data published in the wake of the election.

## Why did Labour lose?

As the clocks chimed 10 p.m. on Thursday 12 December, and polling stations across the nation closed, the results of the exit poll prepared jointly for the BBC, ITV and Sky were broadcast. That poll, constructed on the basis of data taken in 144 carefully selected constituencies, predicted that the Conservatives would secure an overall majority in the Commons, with 368 seats – just three more than they actually achieved when the full results were available the following day (see Table 8.1).

*Table 8.1 2019 general election results (selected parties)*

| Party | Seats | Seats (%) | Votes | Votes (%) |
|---|---|---|---|---|
| Conservative | 365 | 56.2 | 13,966,565 | 43.6 |
| Labour | 202 | 31.1 | 10,269,076 | 32.1 |
| SNP | 48 | 7.4 | 1,242,372 | 3.9 |
| Liberal Democrats | 11 | 1.7 | 3,696,423 | 11.6 |
| DUP | 8 | 1.2 | 244,128 | 0.8 |
| Sinn Féin | 7 | 1.1 | 181,853 | 0.6 |
| Plaid Cymru | 4 | 0.6 | 153,265 | 0.5 |
| SDLP | 2 | 0.3 | 118,737 | 0.4 |
| Green | 1 | 0.2 | 835,579 | 2.7 |
| Alliance | 1 | 0.2 | 134,115 | 0.4 |
| Speaker | 1 | 0.2 | 26,831 | 0.1 |
| Brexit Party | 0 | 0.0 | 642,303 | 2.0 |

Such a catastrophic defeat for the Labour Party led to a good deal of soul-searching, both among leading party figures and within the rank and file. Much of the debate centred on the question of whether party leader Jeremy Corbyn should 'own' the defeat or whether it had instead been a campaign derailed by a single issue, namely Brexit. According to the *Guardian* (see Box 8.1), Labour's defeat resulted from a combination of 'Corbyn's unpopularity, a muddled manifesto, and its Brexit stance'.

### Box 8.1 Five reasons why Labour lost the election

1 Jeremy Corbyn
2 Manifesto
3 Brexit strategy
4 Collapse of Labour's 'red wall'
5 Election strategy

**Source:** *The Guardian*, 13 December 2019

Although Corbyn and his shadow chancellor, John McDonnell, had clearly done their best to set out an ambitious and costed manifesto, it was far too easily portrayed as fanciful and reckless by those on the right – a 'fast-track' back to the 1970s, as a number of commentators quipped. Similarly, while Corbyn was ever-willing to front up and be interrogated on television and radio, something that could not be said of Johnson (who even dodged a set-piece interview with the BBC's Andrew Neil), such events only served to shine a spotlight on the things that were playing against the Labour leader in the press, including claims that he had failed to address anti-Semitism in the party, and his supposed past support for terrorist organisations in Northern Ireland and the Middle East. Although Corbyn's decision to offer a renegotiated Brexit deal and a second referendum, while himself remaining neutral as an honest broker, was probably the only way he could have reconciled what many consider to be his own beliefs with those of others in his party, it lacked the clarity to resist Johnson's simple call to 'Get Brexit done'. Moreover, in trying to bridge the divide within his party, Corbyn only served to further alienate those formerly Labour-voting 'leave' voters living in the constituencies that made up the so-called 'red wall'. The party's election strategy on the ground could also be said to have failed, in that the effort to win marginal seats from the Conservatives had left what had once been Labour safe seats, in areas that had backed Brexit, vulnerable to the Conservative surge.

The failure to mobilise the working classes in support of a Labour programme that was expressly designed with them in mind was stark, with 50% of C2 (skilled manual) workers voting Conservative in post-vote polling undertaken by Lord Ashcroft, compared to just 30% backing Labour (see Table 8.2). This was, of course, the same group that was credited with propelling Margaret Thatcher to successive general election victories in 1979, 1983 and 1987. Indeed, one might also draw a parallel between Labour's left-wing manifesto in the second of those defeats, often dubbed 'the longest suicide note in history', and the programme for government set out by Labour in 2019. Just as Corbyn defended his manifesto in interviews across the weekend of 14–15 December, so too had former Labour leader Michael Foot defended his right to set out what he believed back in 1983, even if it meant losing. While the 2019 Labour manifesto was praised for its honesty in presenting a detailed, radical agenda, it also provided ammunition for those looking to play on voters' fears. This was seen when the Conservative Party HQ's Twitter account was temporarily re-branded to look as though it was a fact-checking account ('FactcheckUK') during the ITV leaders' debate.

***Table 8.2 How Britain voted and why (%)***

| | Conservative | Labour | Liberal Democrat | SNP | Green | Brexit | Other |
|---|---|---|---|---|---|---|---|
| **Total** | 45 | 33 | 12 | 4 | 3 | 2 | 1 |
| **Male** | 48 | 29 | 13 | 4 | 3 | 2 | 1 |
| **Female** | 42 | 36 | 11 | 4 | 3 | 2 | 1 |
| **18–24** | 19 | 57 | 12 | 4 | 5 | 2 | 1 |
| **25–34** | 23 | 55 | 11 | 5 | 3 | 1 | 1 |
| **35–44** | 30 | 45 | 13 | 5 | 4 | 1 | 2 |
| **45–54** | 43 | 35 | 11 | 4 | 3 | 2 | 1 |
| **55–64** | 49 | 27 | 13 | 4 | 3 | 2 | 1 |
| **65+** | 62 | 18 | 12 | 3 | 2 | 2 | 1 |
| **AB** | 44 | 31 | 15 | 4 | 4 | 1 | 1 |
| **C1** | 45 | 33 | 11 | 4 | 3 | 2 | 1 |
| **C2** | 50 | 30 | 9 | 4 | 3 | 2 | 1 |
| **DE** | 43 | 37 | 7 | 4 | 2 | 3 | 1 |

**Source:** Lord Ashcroft polling

However, while Labour's defeat certainly resulted from the interplay between the five factors identified by the *Guardian*, data published by Opinium in the wake of the election left little room for doubt as to where the real problem lay (see Table 8.3). This, remember, was supposedly 'the Brexit election', underlined by the fact that the Brexit Party and the Conservatives, with their relentless 'Get Brexit Done' mantra, did not even turn up to take part in Channel 4's *Britain Decides: Everything But Brexit Debate* on 8 December. The reality, however, was that Jeremy Corbyn was a bigger issue in many voters' minds than that of Brexit.

***Table 8.3 What reasons did people give for not voting Labour?***

| | Main reasons voters did not vote Labour | | |
|---|---|---|---|
| | **Labour's leadership** | **Labour's Brexit position** | **Labour's economic policies** |
| **Did not vote Labour (all)** | 43 | 17 | 12 |
| **Labour defectors (all)** | 37 | 21 | 6 |
| **Labour defectors to Liberal Democrats** | 29 | 15 | 5 |
| **Labour defectors to Conservatives** | 45 | 31 | 6 |

**Source:** Opinium

## What can we learn from the 2019 general election?

It is tempting to conclude that the background to the 2019 general election and the ground over which it was fought are so unique that little, if anything, can be learnt from its outcome. That said, there are a number of points of fact and issues arising that are worthy of mention:

- Labour will have to elect a new leader and establish a new shadow cabinet. In so doing its members will need to decide whether voters were rejecting the personalities or the policies that the party offered up in 2019. Support for 'Corbynism' involved a rejection of the New Labour project. Might the overwhelming rejection of a Corbyn-led Labour Party see a New Labour revival in 2020?
- The Conservative Party will have to find a way of delivering positive benefits to those northern constituencies whose voters have, by the prime minister's own admission, 'lent' their votes to the Conservatives. If he fails to do that, then they will, in all probability, return to the Labour fold at the next election, with Brexit complete and Corbyn having departed the stage.
- Young people are becoming more politically active and are also voting more than in previous decades. Although the Conservatives won the 2019 election by a clear margin on the popular vote, Lord Ashcroft's polling suggests that they were only more popular than Labour with those over the age of 45. Such a demographic will offer hope to the Labour Party as it looks to regroup.

- The first-past-the-post (FPTP) electoral system continues to misrepresent the popular vote. In an age when party loyalties are increasingly fluid, and issues that cut across party lines are very much in vogue, FPTP is also ill suited to provide the required level of voter choice.
- The results of the general election in Scotland and in Northern Ireland have given encouragement to those nationalist parties looking to cut their ties with the UK.
- There are now 220 female MPs, more than ever before (and 34% of the total). The number of black, Asian and minority ethnic (BAME) MPs has also risen, from 52 at the 2017 general election to 65 as 2019 drew to a close. This changing demographic may well have a significant impact on the way in which the Commons operates, especially when one considers some of the backgrounds of the new cohort, and the constituencies that they have been elected to represent.

## Summary

- The 2019 general election was seen as being the fastest way to establish a new government that could command the Commons majority required to end the Brexit stalemate.
- It was made possible by a simple Act of Parliament, the Early Parliamentary General Election Act 2019, which circumvented the Fixed-term Parliaments Act 2011.
- The 2019 general election campaign was one in which the Conservatives focused almost entirely on their mantra of 'Get Brexit done', with Boris Johnson studiously avoiding the kind of close scrutiny to which other main party leaders were subjected.
- Voters appear to have rejected the Labour Party as a result of concerns over the leadership of Jeremy Corbyn, rather than the issue of Brexit, or the party's expansive left-wing manifesto.
- Those favouring Scottish independence and a united Ireland have seen their hands strengthened.
- The House of Commons is becoming increasingly diverse in some respects, with more women and BAME candidates being returned to Westminster.

## How can I use this information in my exam?

Material relating to the 2019 general election can be used across a range of topics. For example, the issue of who has the right to call an election, and when, is relevant to the wider theme of democracy, whereas the more focused section on 'Why did Labour lose?' would be helpful when assessing the impact of campaign strategies. The statistical data provided in this chapter can also be used in a variety of different contexts. Table 8.1, for example, provides good evidence for those seeking to evaluate the fairness of the FPTP electoral system, while the data provided in Tables 8.2 and 8.3 will be useful when studying factors affecting voting behaviour.

## Consolidation activities

1. Produce a detailed spider diagram that sets out the reason why Labour lost the 2019 general election.
2. 'It isn't just about why Labour lost, we should also talk about why the Conservatives won.' Discuss.
3. Study Table 8.1. How could the data in this table be used to argue against the first-past-the-post electoral system? Use figures from the table in support of your answer.
4. Study Table 8.2.
   - a What do these data tell us about how people in different age categories and different social classes voted in 2019?
   - b Is there anything that could be seen as surprising in these data, given what you know already know about voting behaviour?
5. Study the list of consequences set out under the heading 'What can we learn from the 2019 general election?'. Which interests you the most, and why?